General Preface

The object of this series is to provide studies of individual novels, plays and groups of poems and essays which are known to be widely read by students. The emphasis is on clarification and evaluation; biographical and historical facts, while they may be discussed when they throw light on particular elements in a writer's work, are generally subordinated to critical discussion. What kind of work is this? What exactly goes on here? How good is this work, and why? These are the questions that each writer will try to answer.

It should be emphasized that these studies are written on the assumption that the reader has already read carefully the work discussed. The objective is not to enable students to deliver opinions about works they have not read, nor is it to provide ready-made ideas to be applied to works that have been read. In one sense all critical interpretation can be regarded as foisting opinions on readers, but to accept this is to deny the advantages of any sort of critical discussion directed at students or indeed at anybody else. The aim of these studies is to provide what Coleridge called in another context 'aids to reflection' about the works discussed. The interpretations are offered as suggestive rather than as definitive, in the hope of stimulating the reader into developing further his own insights. This is after all the function of all critical discourse among sensible people.

Because of the interest which this kind of study has aroused, it has been decided to extend it first from merely English literature to include also some selected works of American literature and now further to include selected works in English by Commonwealth writers. The criterion will remain that the book studied is important in itself and is widely read by students.

DAVID DAICHES

STUDIES IN ENGLISH LITERATURE No. 19

General Editor

David Daiches

Already published in the series:

1. **Milton:** Comus *and* Samson Agonistes
   by *J. B. Broadbent*
2. **Pope:** The Rape of the Lock
   by *J. S. Cunningham*
3. **Jane Austen:** Emma
   by *Frank Bradbrook*
4. **W. B. Yeats:** The Poems
   by *A. Norman Jeffares*
5. **Chaucer:** The Knight's Tale *and*
   The Clerk's Tale
   by *Elizabeth Salter*
6. **Marlowe:** Dr Faustus
   by *J. P. Brockbank*
7. **Hardy:** The Mayor of Casterbridge
   by *Douglas Brown*
8. **Webster:** The Duchess of Malfi
   by *Clifford Leech*
10. **Wordsworth:** The Prelude and
    other poems by *John F. Danby*
11. **George Eliot:** Middlemarch
    by *David Daiches*
12. **Conrad:** Lord Jim
    by *Tony Tanner*
13. **Shakespeare:** Hamlet
    by *Kenneth Muir*
14. **Shakespeare:** Macbeth
    by *John Russell Brown*
15. **Shakespeare:** King Lear
    by *Nicholas Brooke*
16. **Shakespeare:** Much Ado About Nothing
    by *J. R. Mulryne*
17. **Donne:** Songs and Sonets
    by *A. J. Smith*
18. **Marvell:** Poems
    by *Dennis Davison*
19. **Dickens:** Great Expectations
    by *R. George Thomas*
20. **Emily Brontë:** Wuthering Heights
    by *Frank Goodridge*
21. **Shakespeare:** The Merchant of Venice
    by *A. D. Moody*

22. **Tennyson:** In Memoriam
    by *K. W. Gransden*
23. **Fielding:** Tom Jones
    by *I. Ehrenpreis*
24. **Shakespeare:** Henry IV
    by *R. J. Beck*
25. **Shakespeare:** As You Like It
    by *Michael Jamieson*
26. **Shakespeare:** The Winter's Tale
    by *A. D. Nuttall*
28. **D. H. Lawrence:** Sons and Lovers
    by *Gāmini Salgādo*
29. **Dickens:** Little Dorrit
    by *J. C. Reid*
30. **E. M. Forster:** A Passage to India
    by *John Colmer*
31. **Shakespeare:** Richard II
    by *A. R. Humphreys*
32. **Henry James:** The Portrait of a Lady
    by *David Galloway*
33. **Gissing:** New Grub Street
    by *P. J. Keating*
34. **Blake:** The Lyric Poetry
    by *John Holloway*
35. **Shakespeare:** A Midsummer Night's
    Dream
    by *Stephen Fender*
36. **Mark Twain:** Huckleberry Finn
    by *Jonathan Raban*
37. **T. S. Eliot:** The Waste Land
    by *Helen Williams (2nd edition)*
38. **Swift:** Gulliver's Travels
    by *Angus Ross*
39. **Shakespeare:** The Tempest
    by *John Russell Brown*
40. **Conrad:** Nostromo
    by *Juliet McLauchlan*
41. **Tennyson:** The Early Poems
    by *John Pettigrew*
42. **Golding:** Lord of the Flies
    by *John S. Whitley*

Already published in the series (*continued*):

CHARLES DICKENS:
GREAT EXPECTATIONS

by

R. GEORGE THOMAS

Professor of English
University College, Cardiff

EDWARD ARNOLD

41478

First published 1964
by Edward Arnold (Publishers) Ltd
41 Bedford Square, London WC1B 3DQ

Reprinted 1966, 1968, 1971, 1977, 1979

ISBN: 0 7131 5089 0

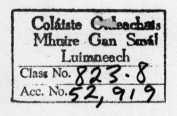
Printed and bound in Great Britain at
The Camelot Press Ltd, Southampton

Contents

For Edward G. Cox
and E. C. Llewellyn

Introductory

Great Expectations first appeared in weekly parts in Dickens's second periodical, *All the Year Round*; it ran from December 1860 until June 1861 and was subsequently issued in three volumes in the autumn of 1861, a few weeks before Dickens set out on his second tour of public readings from his works. Like *A Tale of Two Cities*, which also appeared in *All the Year Round*, *Great Expectations* is about two-thirds of the length of the other major novels, all of which were designed for monthly publication in twenty parts before they were issued as single works. Neither the weekly serial nor the first three-volume edition of *Great Expectations* was illustrated. Yet another distinguishing mark, which it also shares with *A Tale of Two Cities*, is the absence of any detailed memoranda about the novel's progress. Beginning with *Martin Chuzzlewit*, the initial composition of which had caused him considerable trouble and which marks the end of his first period of copious and felicitous writing, Dickens paid more attention to the forward planning of his novels and kept notes (still extant) in order 'to keep a steadier eye upon the general purpose and design'. There are no sketch notes for any individual numbers of *Great Expectations*; the notes which survive contain some detailed calculations about the ages of the ten chief characters, a calculation on the state of the tides on the Thames, and a sketch of the conclusion of the novel. These notes were drawn up after Chapter 42 (the story of Magwitch's life) was written and were designed to cover the last six chapters of the novel. They certainly throw no light on the original pattern of the story, although they give ample illustration of the firm measure of planned control which Dickens exercised over his tale. These notes also remind us of some of the difficulties inherent in the method of serial publication and of the special problem that often faced Dickens in rounding off his novels: a subject that cannot be avoided in discussing *Great Expectations* for which two endings were provided.

Fortunately John Forster, the novelist's friend, adviser, and correspondent, has recorded the genesis of the novel in some detail in *The Life of Charles Dickens*. In October 1860, Forster suggested that Dickens should 'let himself loose upon some single humorous conception in the vein of his youthful achievements in that way'. Relevant extracts from Dickens's replies made the next week are as follows:

'For a little piece I have been writing—or am writing; for I hope to finish it today—such a very fine, new, and grotesque idea has opened upon me, that I begin to doubt whether I had not better cancel the little paper and reserve the notion for a new book. You shall judge as soon as I get it printed. But it so opens out before *me* that I can see the whole of a serial revolving on it, in a most singular and comic manner.

'Last week I got to work on the new story. I had previously very carefully considered the state and prospects of *All the Year Round*, and, the more I considered them, the less hope I saw of being able to get back, now, to the profit of a separate publication [i.e. of *Great Expectations*] in the old 20 numbers. . . . I have therefore decided to begin the story as of the length of the *Tale of Two Cities* on the first of December— begin publishing, that is. I must make the most I can out of the book. You shall have the first two or three weekly parts tomorrow. The name is GREAT EXPECTATIONS. I think a good name?

'The book will be written in the first person throughout, and during these first three weekly numbers you will find the hero to be a boy-child, like David. I have made the opening, I hope, in its general effect exceedingly droll. I have put a child and a good-natured foolish man, in relations that seem to me very funny. Of course I have got in the pivot on which the story will turn too—and which indeed, as you remember, was the grotesque tragi-comic conception that first en-couraged me. To be quite sure I had fallen into no unconscious repeti-tions, I read *David Copperfield* again the other day, and was affected by it to a degree you would hardly believe.

'It is a pity that the third portion [i.e. from Chapter 40 of the novel] cannot be read all at once, because its purpose would be much more apparent; and the pity is the greater, because the general turn and tone of the working out and winding up, will be away from all such things as they conventionally go. But what must be, must be. As to the planning out from week to week, nobody can imagine what the difficulty is, without trying. But, as in all such cases, when it is overcome the pleasure is proportionate. Two months more will see me through it, I trust. All the iron is in the fire, and I have "only" to beat it out.

'You will be surprised to hear that I have changed the end of *Great Expectations* from and after Pip's return to Joe's, and finding his little likeness there. Bulwer [Lytton], who has been, as I think you know, extraordinarily taken by the book, so strongly urged it upon me, after reading the proofs, and supported his view with such good reasons, that I resolved to make the change. You shall have it when you come back to town. I have put in as pretty a little piece of writing as I could, and I have no doubt the story will be more acceptable through the alteration.'

When *Great Expectations* was written Dickens was a very rich man but the novel does not give a rosy picture of a life of wealth. The middle fifties of the nineteenth century were critical years for Dickens's social thinking and this novel followed *Dombey and Son*, *Bleak House*, *Little Dorrit* and *Our Mutual Friend* in which Dickens tried 'with increasing success to create a vivid vision of society that would be at once extensive and comprehensive'. (Monroe Engel, *The Maturity of Dickens*, 1959.) Engel sees a difference in tone and approach between the two novels in which Dickens explored his 'sense of self', *David Copperfield* (1850) and *Great Expectations* ten years later: the former is a success story told in such a way that the pathos of the upward struggle of David remains uppermost in the reader's mind; whereas *Great Expectations* describes 'a movement away from success, and its dominant mood is ironic'. Though I agree with the view that *David Copperfield* is closer to our fuller understanding of Dickens's inner life than most of his novels, my many readings of *Great Expectations* have confirmed me in the opinion that the later novel is almost a model paradigm of Dickens's powerful response to the needs and aspirations of his own reading public. This later novel was written between the first and second of the novelist's lecture tours during which he read from his writings to large audiences and first tasted the power of his personal magnetism over crowds of devoted admirers. There is a sense in which Dickens has succeeded in *Great Expectations* in recapturing the lost art of the Icelandic writers of the Family Sagas—their ability 'to make books talk'. And though the analyses that follow in this study will try to lay bare the raw material and the varied techniques out of which Pip's story was constructed, this abiding sense of the uniform voice of the narrator (or is it the author?) remains once the novel is picked up and read through for enjoyment alone.

1. The Story, Plot, or Fable

Great Expectations was originally conceived as a 'grotesque, tragi-comic', long short-story. Very quickly, and in answer to the obvious need for a popular serial that would increase the falling sales of *All the Year Round*, it developed into a serial of weekly instalments that fully satisfied the taste of Dickens's weekly readers. In addition, this hastily expanded novel strengthened Dickens's standing as a novelist among the more critical readers of his day. Carlyle, it is true, thought it worth 'a penny to read before going to bed' and thoroughly enjoyed 'that Pip nonsense' which had sent him into roars of laughter. An anonymous reviewer in the *Saturday Review*, who had severely attacked some earlier novels, recognised that with *Great Expectations* Dickens had returned to his best vein, as exemplified by *Martin Chuzzlewit* and *David Copperfield*.

During the ten years before 1860, Dickens, as well as his critics, appeared to be more conscious of the technique of novel-writing and *Great Expectations* benefits considerably from a tighter plot-contrivance and a more closely organised and interwoven structure, than, say, *Pickwick Papers* or *Oliver Twist*.

The major structural feature of the novel is its division into the three distinct 'stages of Pip's Expectations'. The use of the word 'stage' is itself a suggestive one: it combines the notion of stages on a journey—so essential to any understanding of the pre-twentieth-century novel—with a suggestion of the theatre. Pip's progress from industrious obscurity, through wilful public idleness, to a resigned, yet modest acceptance of his true place in society is an obvious variation on the picaresque theme and carries with it many of the significant overtones of earlier picaresque novels. His progress, however, is rounded and compressed within three acts with a tightness of structure and a closeness of cross-reference that were rarely found in the private theatricals that then occupied Dickens's leisure. The clearest parallels to this dramatic division can be found in the novels of Jane Austen and in *Wuthering Heights*.

Dickens appears to be very conscious of the need to 'bring down the curtain' at the end of each 'stage' with a significant piece of writing. His sense of theatre was highly developed; the need for a flourish would have come very easily to him: Stage One ends (Chapter 19) with a faint suggestion of Adam and Eve leaving the Garden of Eden:

'We changed again, and yet again, and it was now too late and too far to go back, and I went on. And the mists had all solemnly risen now, and the world lay spread before me.'[1]

The penultimate paragraph is even more skilfully contrived as a running commentary on the state of the 'action' at this final moment in the first act:

'So subdued I was by those tears, and by their breaking out again in the course of the quiet walk, that when I was on the coach, and it was clear of the town, I deliberated with an aching heart whether I would not get down when we changed horses and walk back, and have another evening at home, and a better parting. We changed, and I had not made up my mind, and still reflected for my comfort that it would be quite practicable to get down and walk back, when we changed again. And while I was occupied with those deliberations, I would fancy an exact resemblance to Joe in some man coming along the road towards us, and my heart would beat high.—As if he could possibly be there!' As we read, the adult Pip, the narrator, is forgotten; probably because the contrasting ideas of forward motion and retrogression are sharply emphasised in the verbs. The desire to 'get down and walk back' is closely linked both with the word 'change' and the fanciful idea that Joe is walking out of the past to meet Pip at this decisive stage in his expectations. And then suddenly the narrator takes charge in the continuous present tense ('As if he could possibly be there!') and terminates the moment of hesitancy. The final paragraph brings down the curtain with an echo of the 'mists that were solemnly rising' when Pip had left the village where he 'had been so innocent'.

The end of the second stage of Pip's expectations (Chapter 39) is described in nine short paragraphs. They are designed to sum up the entire action of the novel (in so far as it concerns Pip's inner biography) up to this point when the curtain is lowered on this moment of despair and ruin in his fortunes: 'the clocks of the Eastward churches were striking five, the candles were wasted out, the fire was dead, and the wind and rain intensified the thick black darkness'. The passage is skilfully contrived. Pip and Magwitch are cut off from the world like two

[1] All quotations from the novel are taken from *Great Expectations*, The New Oxford Illustrated Dickens, 1953.

characters imprisoned within a stage set. The shutters are drawn and communication with all other characters is at an end; Magwitch brings into the room all the old eating habits of the escaped convict until Pip is left up centre stage with his memories of Miss Havisham, Estella, the Old Bailey, Herbert, Joe and Biddy. Even a faint suggestion of super-natural promptings and forebodings are given in order to emphasise Pip's loneliness and sense of isolation: 'With these fears upon me, I began either to imagine or recall that I had had mysterious warnings of this man's approach. . . . That, his wicked spirit had somehow sent these messengers to mine, and that now on this stormy night he was as good as his word, and with me.' Pip's final attempt to break the tension of his bad dream by taking one last look at his 'dreadful burden' has its own theatrical quality and the sleeping ex-convict is presented to the reader in the close-up manner of Dickens's usual reliance on vividly detailed description: 'He had rolled a handkerchief round his head, and his face was set and lowering in his sleep.' Inevitably, and melodramat-ically, 'he had a pistol lying on the pillow'.

Professors John Butt and Kathleen Tillotson have noted that Dickens experienced considerable difficulty in writing some of the last double numbers which concluded his monthly instalments; his notebooks for *Dombey and Son*, *David Copperfield* and *Little Dorrit* are thick with jottings at this point. The notes for *Great Expectations* seem to have been written after Chapter 43 and were apparently designed to maintain the pattern of the story unchanged throughout the last six chapters. Leaving aside for the present any discussion of the alternative endings and accepting the end as Dickens published it, we can see that Dickens still thought of the ending of this third and final stage in theatrical terms. All the minor characters are suitably paired off or dismissed from the action with a characteristic gesture: Satis House is pulled down; Herbert and Clara, like Biddy and Joe, are married; only the Blue Boar Inn, the Forge, the mist, the churchyard, and the deserted garden remain unchanged and unaltered. The marshes, the hulks, the traces and echoes of crime and punishment are replaced by the newly emerging life of another young Pip and the final, subdued meeting of Pip and Estella. In echoic fashion, the third stage—this time a stage on a journey that will continue after the novel is ended—recaptures the mood and the terms of reference of the end of the first stage of Pip's expectations:

'I took her hand in mine, and we went out of the ruined place; and, as the morning mists had risen long ago when I first left the forge, so, the evening mists were rising now, and in all the broad expanse of tranquil light they showed to me, I saw no shadow of another parting from her.'

Theatrical methods are also used by Dickens in the main body of his narrative. In all his novels he relies on set scenes that are almost ready to be transported to the stage. During the last decade Mr. Emlyn Williams, following Dickens's own example on his successful reading tours, has demonstrated the ease with which selected scenes from the novels can yield the raw material for a whole evening's entertainment in the theatre. *Great Expectations* abounds in such potentially 'dramatic sketches' between two speakers.

In the majority of instances these scenes are brief: Pip and the convict (Chapter 3), Pip and Joe (7); Joe, his wife, and Orlick (15); Mr. Wopsle and Mr. Jaggers (18). But occasionally in the later part of the novel such stage scenes are extended in scope, range and dramatic intensity until the reader can imagine that he is sitting in the wings or is present at a dress rehearsal. There are two memorable scenes of this nature. In Chapter 38 Pip's dreams of wealth and expectation are about to collapse with the return of Magwitch. One shaky prop in this fanciful super-structure was his belief that Estella would eventually become his wife. The entire chapter is designed to destroy this illusion and to force Pip to see through both the character of Miss Havisham and the uncertain foundations for his own wild dreams. His moment of revelation is first presented to the reader as autobiographical recollection:

'I saw in this, wretched though it made me, and bitter the sense of dependence, even of degradation, that it awakened—I saw in this, that Estella was set to wreak Miss Havisham's revenge on men, and that she was not to be given to me until she had gratified it for a term I saw in this, a reason for her being beforehand assigned to me. Sending her out to attract and torment and do mischief, Miss Havisham sent her with the malicious assurance that she was beyond the reach of all admirers, and that all who staked upon that cast were secured to lose. I saw in this, that I, too, was tormented by a perversion of ingenuity, even while the prize was reserved for me. I saw in this, the reason for my being staved off so long, and the reason for my late guardian's declining to commit himself to the formal knowledge of such a scheme. In a word, I saw in this, Miss Havisham as I had her then and there before my eyes, and always had had her before my eyes; and I saw in this, the distinct shadow of the darkened and unhealthy house in which her life was hidden from the sun.

'The candles that lighted that room of hers were placed in sconces on the wall. They were high from the ground, and they burnt with the steady dullness of artificial light in air that is seldom renewed. As I looked round at them, and at the pale gloom they made, and at the stopped clock, and at the withered articles of bridal dress upon the table and the ground, and at her own awful figure with its ghostly reflection thrown large by the fire upon the ceiling and the wall, I saw in everything the construction that my mind had come to, repeated and thrown back to me. My thoughts passed into the great room across the landing where the table was spread, and I saw it written, as it were, in the falls of the cobwebs from the centrepiece, in the crawlings of the spiders on the cloth, in the tracks of the mice as they betook their little quickened hearts behind the panels, and in the gropings and pausings of the beetles on the floor.'

So far Dickens relies heavily on the visual recreation of the details of the seen (e.g. the repetition of 'I saw'); but as Pip continues to stare at the two women, the scene becomes a theatre and the tensions inherent in the relationship between them are brought to a verbal climax in the following dialogue:

' "Did I never give her love!" cried Miss Havisham, turning wildly to me. "Did I never give her a burning love, inseparable from jealousy at all times, and from sharp pain, while she speaks thus to me! Let her call me mad, let her call me mad!"

' "Why should I call you mad," returned Estella, "I, of all people? Does any one live, who knows what set purposes you have, half as well as I do? Does any one live, who knows what a steady memory you have, half as well as I do? I who have sat on this same hearth on the little stool that is even now beside you there, learning your lessons and looking up into your face, when your face was strange and frightened me!"

' "Soon forgotten!" moaned Miss Havisham. "Times soon forgotten!"

' "No, not forgotten," retorted Estella. "Not forgotten, but treasured up in my memory. When have you found me false to your teaching? When have you found me unmindful of your lessons? When have you found me giving admission here," she touched her bosom with her hand, "to anything that you excluded? Be just to me."

' "So proud, so proud!" moaned Miss Havisham, pushing away her grey hair with both her hands.

' "Who taught me to be proud?" returned Estella. "Who praised me when I learnt my lesson?"

' "So hard, so hard!" moaned Miss Havisham, with her former action.

' "Who taught me to be hard?" returned Estella. "Who praised me when I learnt my lesson?"

' "But to be proud and hard to *me*!" Miss Havisham quite shrieked, as she stretched out her arms. "Estella, Estella, Estella, to be proud and hard to *me*!"

'Estella looked at her for a moment with a kind of calm wonder, but was not otherwise disturbed; when the moment was passed, she looked down at the fire again.

' "I cannot think," said Estella, raising her eyes after a silence, "why you should be so unreasonable when I come to see you after a separation. I have never forgotten your wrongs and their causes. I have never been unfaithful to you or your schooling. I have never shown any weakness that I can charge myself with."

' "Would it be weakness to return my love?" exclaimed Miss Havisham. "But yes, yes, she would call it so!"

' "I begin to think," said Estella, in a musing way, after another moment of calm wonder, "that I almost understand how this comes about. If you had brought up your adopted daughter wholly in the dark confinement of these rooms, and had never let her know that there was such a thing as the daylight by which she has never once seen your face—if you had done that, and then, for a purpose, had wanted her to understand the daylight and know all about it, you would have been disappointed and angry?"

'Miss Havisham, with her head in her hands, sat making a low moaning, and swaying herself on her chair, but gave no answer.

' "Or," said Estella, "—which is a nearer case—if you had taught her, from the dawn of her intelligence, with your utmost energy and might, that there was such a thing as daylight, but that it was made to be her enemy and destroyer, and she must always turn against it, for it had blighted you and would else blight her;—if you had done this, and then, for a purpose, had wanted her to take naturally to the daylight and she could not do it, you would have been disappointed and angry?"

'Miss Havisham sat listening (or it seemed so, for I could not see her face), but still made no answer.

' "So," said Estella, "I must be taken as I have been made. The success is not mine, the failure is not mine, but the two together make me." '

As the scene ends Pip decides to leave the room and, as he looks back, we are supplied with a final view of the stage set as the curtain comes down: 'When I left, Estella was yet standing by the great chimney-piece, just as she had stood throughout. Miss Havisham's grey hair was all adrift upon the ground, among the other bridal wrecks, and was a miserable sight to see.'

The second scene of extended stage dialogue is in chapter 50, when Herbert informs Pip of Provis's story about his child. The entire chapter —a very short one—shows quite clearly that Dickens was in complete control of his narrative. Pip's hands and arms are bandaged after the fire at Satis House and in the first two paragraphs the reader's attention is directed toward's Pip's acute suffering. When he dozes off the details of the fire are recalled vividly, in his dreams; when he awakens, the unspoken problem of Provis's safety is hinted at. 'But then, as Herbert changed the bandages, more by the light of the fire than by the outer light, he went back to it spontaneously. "I sat with Provis last night, Handel, two good hours." ' The stage has been set—even the lighting has been suggested—and the dialogue continues for three pages until the rather melodramatic last line is spoken by Pip:

' "I know I am quite myself. And the man we have in hiding down the river is Estella's Father." '

There is no need to illustrate the point further, but the student will find for himself at least a dozen other scenes in the novel—including nearly all those which involve Mr. Jaggers—that demonstrate Dickens' constant reliance on such theatrical set pieces both to enliven the flow of his narrative and to concentrate the moments of high tension into memorable dialogue.

Great Expectations illustrates no single theory of narrative construction. Dickens employs a mixed form which embraces the best qualities and methods found in the practice of earlier novelists and in his own earlier successful novels. The ingredients are many and varied, but no set recipe emerges. Dickens's earlier exuberance of comic invention, both in situation and dialogue, is now less spontaneous and this is to be expected from so prolific a writer and public speaker. Yet at no time did the fountain of humour run dry and in *Great Expectations* the comic scenes are successfully integrated into the general purpose of the story. There is some difference in their employment between the first 'stage' and the other two, and many characters (e.g. Pumblechook, Wopsle and, to some extent, Wemmick) undergo a subtle change as the novel progresses. Conceived originally, one suspects, in the Pickwickian fantastic sense, the comic characters are later used to further the story, to unravel entanglements in the plot, or even to round out the many half-hidden themes that lie just below the surface of the plain narrative. A few set-pieces remain: Pip's sister 'on the Rampage'; Mr. Wopsle's reading of *George Barnwell* (Chapter 15); Mr. Pumblechook's 'May I' (Chapter 19); Pip's introduction to the family of Mr. Matthew Pocket (Chapters 22, 23); the behaviour of Trabb's boy (Chapter 30); and some of the encounters at Walworth with, as a final *tour de force*, the wedding of Wemmick and Miss Skiffins (Chapter 55). Such comic scenes, which are developed solely for their own intrinsic comic worth, become rarer as the story advances towards its climax. Wemmick disappears from the novel one chapter before Magwitch dies and, as the story returns more closely to its village origins, Joe and Pumblechook are left to supply the comedy in a slightly altered key.

A third and vestigial narrative method employed in the novel is the 'inset story' which was so frequently used by those eighteenth-century novelists which the young Dickens had read so eagerly. The most significant is Magwitch's story of his life (Chapter 42). Despite the 'low' style in which it is narrated, Magwitch's story ('put at once into a mouthful of English') is a *reductio ad absurdum* of all the picaresque tales ever told in English or French novels: 'In jail and out of jail, in jail and out of jail, in jail and out of jail.' But this is no mere device adopted by Dickens mechanically or unthinkingly. In *Great Expectations* the numerous flash-back narratives certainly clarify some of the mysteries inherent in the plot; they also help to thicken the sense of 'time past' converging upon and dominating 'time present'. The device is absorbed into the thematic as well as the structural pattern of the autobiography or *Bildungsroman*. As the third 'stage' is unfolded before him, the reader becomes conscious of the consummate skill with which the narrator is re-living the past as he tells it. In this carefully organised approach to a unitary narrative, the 'inset-tales' are utilised to give the sense of pre-destined events that somehow condition Pip's behaviour without excusing it. The approach to the past is impersonal and our attention is concentrated upon the events; we react to the fate of the teller at a distance which is one remove from the incidents themselves, which are filtered through to us by hindsight and retrospection. By contrast, the barbarous dialect which Dickens puts into Magwitch's mouth, and the occasional descriptions of his coarse manners which interrupt the narrative, help to concentrate our attention on Magwitch not only as he lived through these long past events but also as they have affected the rest of his life. Dickens is employing a double perspective and, in the process, he brings the climax of his tale one step nearer and makes it more credible. When the narrative is over, the reader has shared, if only temporarily, the convict's ingrained hatred for Compeyson. The barbarous fight in the ditch (from Chapter 5) invades the upper room in Barnard's Inn where the two young city gentlemen are listening and casts its shadow forward towards the locked death-struggle with Compeyson in the Thames at the end of Chapter 54. In seven pages Dickens has tightened the threads of his narrative, darkened the easy-going life of two young men with memories of a world quite distinct from their own, and released into the drawing-room, dream-like world of Pip's second 'stage' those pent-up forces of the picaro life of rogues and vagabonds which lie below and just beyond the pale of respectable organised society and which, at any moment of crisis, threaten to rise and destroy it. Carlyle, the historian of the French Revolution, may have laughed at that 'Pip nonsense'; Magwitch's life-story darkens the nonsense with overtones from *A Tale of Two Cities* and the underworld of Victorian London.

The structural patterns in *Great Expectations* have been analysed in some detail by John H. Hagan (*E.L.H.*, XXI, 1; 1954). After referring to the most conspicuous artistry with which 'the story has been organised into three large sections of virtually equal length' which correspond in 'moral or temporal terms' to phases of Boyhood, Youth and Maturity, Mr. Hagan points out that each one of the stages 'has its various sub-divisions, no less evident because they go without explicit mention'. Stage One is divided into four subdivisions: Chapters 1-6, 7-11, 12-17 and 18-19. Stage Two's subdivisions are Chapters 20-27, 28-35, and

36-39; those for Stage Three are Chapters 40-46, 47-51, 52-56 and 57-59. Consciously, or unconsciously, Dickens has imposed on his novel a balancing external appearance of symmetry which becomes even more significant when the various subdivisions are regarded as reflecting images balanced around the central point of the narrative. Mr. Hagan's analysis should be read in full but the following examples will suggest the nature of his argument. Chapters 1-6 contain Pip's first encounter with the convict; Chapters 40-46 are devoted to their second meeting; Chapters 7-11, in which Pip is first introduced to Miss Havisham and Estella, are balanced against Chapters 47-51 where Miss Havisham's nature begins to alter and Estella's parentage is revealed; Pip's departure from the old Forge (Chapters 18-19) is balanced by his return there as an experienced, disillusioned man in Chapters 57-59. In other words, each subdivision in the first Stage of Pip's expectations is balanced, fulfilled and completed by the corresponding section in the third Stage.

This is no mere act of mechanical balancing. The successive stages in the growth of Pip's expectations develop gradually but perceptibly from Pip's own acts of deceit. He lies about the file and the food out of terror and sheer fright, but his fanciful embroidering of his visit to Satis House is a conscious and calculated act of deception with deep roots in snobbery and class-consciousness. From this moment onwards the graph of his own capacity for self-deceit can be easily drawn until it culminates in the advent of Jaggers and the fortuitous connection between Miss Havisham, Pip, Jaggers and the 'great expectations'. But, even then, all the links in this hidden chain of chance, deceit, circum-spection, hypocrisy, snobbery, crime and mania have not been fully uncovered. With sure skill and fine economy Dickens advances his story within a vast interlocking series of events that must wait upon time, memory, recollection and revelation before their unseen tangles are made clear in the last and third Stage. Pip's rise to a position of unstable prosperity, balanced as it was on a series of progressive acts of self-deceit, is counterbalanced by his final return to the workaday world of hard work and honest reward which is achieved through a series of acts of clear vision and knowledge not only about his own nature but also about all the characters who have come to form the society in which he lives out his life of easy expectancy.

In retrospect one is surprised at the small number of minor characters in the novel and even more surprised at the even smaller number who have no connection at all with the main story except at one point. The careful balancing of incident between the first and third Stages is paralleled in the multiple functions of secondary characters like Wopsle, Orlick, Drummle, Startop and Pumblechook who double up their parts with the same skill—and, perhaps, the same show of contrivance— that characterises Mr. Wopsle's theatrical performances in London. Eventually, of course, the number of actors is reduced until the intimate circle of Joe, Mrs. Joe and Pip is re-created in the home of Joe, Biddy and *their* child, Pip, who is no longer an orphan but the happy offspring of a genuine marriage of affection.

Enough has been said—though one tithe of the possible illustration of these repetitive patterns has been used above—to suggest the close fidelity with which Dickens has organised his plot material around a few central ideas and incidents. It would be a gross misrepresentation of the novel's scope to maintain that anything like a fraction of Pip's expectations are ever realised in terms of narrative adventure, width of scene, or breadth of social intercourse. The social boundaries of the novel are quite narrow. Estella and Drummle, Mrs. Pocket and Mrs. Brandley, supply faint lines of communication to a slightly more genteel world than that of Pumblechook and Wemmick; the locale of the rest of the novel is shadowy and ill-defined, except where it is fantastic, sordid or rural. Nor, except for the sudden spurts of action as the climax approaches, is the action of the story carried forward on the open, classless road so beloved by Smollett and Fielding. There are still a few carefully observed road journeys in *Great Expectations* and, offstage, we are informed of the wanderings of Magwitch and Compeyson, Provis's life in Australia, and the activities of Clarriker and Co. 'in the East', but my residual memory of the story is of long journeys on foot inter-spersed with the sudden culminating incidents on the Thames. By confining the social and spatial boundaries of his story, Dickens was left free to explore Pip's memories in depth—particularly those half-recollected depths of memory that rise, at first, haphazardly to the sur-face of consciousness before the full flood of more detailed, inter-connected incidents can lay bare the springs of conduct and choice. Any close analysis of the novel's structure may possibly give the im-pression that Dickens has manipulated his plot to good effect. This is not the impression left by a re-reading of the novel: it has a thoroughly satisfying sense of rounded completeness and organic unity.

Dickens was not careless about the treatment of time in *Great Expectations*. (As we have seen above, his few extant notes about the novel contain much about the ages of his chief characters.) Like Scott, Thackeray, George Eliot and the Brontës, Dickens tried to set the action of most of his novels vaguely within living memory and although, as Humphrey House and others have pointed out, he was not always careful in his back-dating, his addiction to the Age of the Coach (just prior to the Railway Age) freed his novels from any suggestion of a distant, romantic past while allowing to the novelist a free hand in the invention of realistic and verifiable settings. Miss Mary Edminson has shown ('The Date of the Action of *Great Expectations*', *N.C.F.*, XIII, 1958) that the main action of this novel is established 'within a definite period, with great care'. The convicts' hulks were condemned in 1847; Pip uses flint and steel (before the first 'lucifer' was invented in 1827) when he was 7 years old; in Chapter 46 there is a reference to the Old London Bridge which was finally replaced in August 1831, so that Pip was 23 some time before that date; Wemmick's Catalogue of six Bridges (Chapter 36) contains none opened after 1819 so that Pip cannot be 21 before 1819; two references, to paddle steamers (Chapter 54) and to the restricted use of steam navigation before the early 1840s, suggest a date for the attempted escape abroad with Magwitch at a time close to 1824. Miss Edminson's evidence indicates that the main action of the story was enacted between 1807 (or 1810) and 1823 (or 1826). Many other details, woven almost casually into the text, support this assumption. On his return Magwitch is dressed in 'shorts', a slang term for breeches that went out of fashion around 1815; gas light was introduced in 1807 but was not in general use before the period 1814-20; transportation to New South Wales was discontinued in 1840. In fact, Dickens was as consistent about the temporal setting of the action as he was about the internal dating and causal relationships of the internal action of his story. He appears to have taken great pains to remove his story from the area of contemporary observation—if not of possible living memory—and so to concentrate any social criticism implicit in his tale against the more timeless defects in human society which arise when moral values and social aspirations have gone astray.

More pertinently for any analysis of the structure of *Great Expectations* is the validity with which this careful temporal setting invests the auto-biographical recollections of Pip the narrator whose story we are reading. If we can trust Pip's recollection of things past when his word can be checked against folk-memory or historical records, then surely—we are forced to conclude—we may accept him as a reasonably honest and reliable interpreter of his own feelings and attitudes towards the highly personal, introspective actions that he records. Dickens re-read *David Copperfield* as Pip's story was being shaped in order to avoid unnecessary plagiarism or repetition. We also know that David's tale often comes very close to Dickens's own autobiography: indeed, large sections of the earlier novel are so compulsively written that the reader can neither put it down nor fail to hear the very voice of the author (narrator) speaking. There is none of this attention-compelling prose in Pip's recollections; instead we accept its cool veracity and follow the narration with a genuine, yet uncommitted concern for the outcome of events. We believe in them without being forcibly held by an Ancient-Mariner-like hypnosis. The difference between the two novels, in this respect at least, is a measure of Dickens's great care to ground Pip's life-story on externally verifiable facts that would cast an aura of truthfulness over the more imaginative (and personally tender) sections of the novel.

It would be surprising if Dickens's imposition of fixed temporal limits on Pip's story, however apposite a reflection of the narrator's very act of recollection it proved to be, were to result in a weakening of the sense of place within the novel as a whole.

A significant part of *Great Expectations* is presented to us in dramatic scenes and in long snatches of dramatic dialogue, but not at the expense of the usual, detailed Dickensian description of the localities and 'sets' against which the action takes place. For, as George Orwell and others have emphasised, Dickens's imaginative reconstruction of the world of experience is marked by his close attention to observed details: his art, even at its most fantastic point, is an extension of his amazingly gifted reporter's eye. In other words, it is impossible to imagine a novel by Dickens, however controlled and centrally organised in the service of a single dominating theme, that does not pay close attention to the locale in which the action is carried out. So that just as the stage-like scenes and passages of rapid dialogue suspend the forward drive of the plot for a time, and incidentally provide moments of rest, the passages of set description can also give their own points of rest and timelessness within the framework of the fast-moving narrative. At such moments,

for example the visits to Walworth or Newgate, the first introduction
to the home of Matthew Pocket, the meeting with Drummle at the Blue
Boar, the restless night spent at Hummums, the walk to Chinks's Basin
along the Old Green Copper Rope-Walk, the taut scene at the Sessions,
—and numerous other passages scattered throughout the novel—Dickens
seems to be broadening his canvas rather than advancing his story.
There is undoubtedly a fast-moving tale, carefully set in place and time,
which takes place between Pip's seventh and twenty-third birthdays;
there is also a sense in which the entire novel is constructed like a series
of radiating spokes which move away from a single remembered experience and which are held in place and perspective by the fully-rounded
circumferential knowledge of the mature Pip. And this knowledge is
shared with the reader when the last stage of Pip's expectations is
reached. In his perceptive study of 'Dickens and the Sense of Time'
(*N.C.F.*, XIII, 1958), Mr. John H. Raleigh argues that in both *David
Copperfield* and *Great Expectations* the 'idea of existence in time as a
compound of memory and desire' is added to 'the temporal implications
of the involved plotting'. Mr. Raleigh finds that generally in the novels
of Dickens there are two plot lines: one on the surface and one which is
either hinted at or completely submerged. Certainly, the care taken by
Dickens to present acceptable times and places for *Great Expectations*
arose from an instinct deeper than the serial plotter's desire for a superficial tidiness: his concern with the numerical aspects of time is paralleled
by a wider concern with the place of chance, pre-destination and
maturity in the life-patterns of his four principal characters, Pip, Estella,
Magwitch and Miss Havisham.

Pip's story has many overtones precisely because the elements from
so many different kinds of story-teller have gone into its telling. Sir
Philip Sidney's apology for poetry can be extended to include Dickens's
novel: 'If then a man can arrive, at that child's age to know that the
poets' persons and doings are but pictures what should be, and not
stories what have been, they will never give the lie to things not affirm-
atively but allegorically and figuratively written. And therefore, as in
History looking for truth, they go away full fraught with falsehood, so
in Poesy, looking for fiction, they shall use the narration but as an
imaginative ground-plot of a profitable invention.' The imaginative
ground-plot of *Great Expectations* is a fairy-tale adjusted to the taste
and needs of the mature, adult mind: it caters for an adult sense of

disillusionment with the haphazard gifts of Fortune and, at the same time, it feeds the subconscious desires and dreams of all men for a perfectionist world, an Earthly Paradise in which magic has its place and where transformation episodes (like Pip's change from the Forge to a gentleman) can really come to pass. For it is part of Dickens's strength as a novelist that, although his clear perception of certain social evils lies at the heart of his more sombre later novels, he never lost sight of the 'vision splendid'.

To achieve this double vision Dickens employed multiple and diverse techniques of story-telling. The majestically controlled account of Magwitch's final attempt at escape (Chapter 54) must be balanced against the melodramatic poverty of Orlick's attempted murder in the previous chapter; Miss Havisham's credible, psycho-pathological way of life must be accepted along with the rather shadowy life lived by Mr. Jaggers' ex-murderess housekeeper; one's rounded affection for Joe, as for someone in real life, is as much part of the novel as one's rather detached, tolerant, yet humorous acceptance of the way Dickens allows Wemmick, Aged P and Miss Skiffins to go through their Punch-and-Judy show for our delectation. The freedom and pace of genuine picaresque sequences are as essential to the novel as the stage-like scenes and the impassioned descriptions of time and place. A few sentimental passages, and one or two pieces of direct address to the reader, interrupt the flow of the narrative and jar on our contemporary sense of fitness in the reader-author relationship. But even these are caught up into the action of the story which never flags because at all times Dickens is either leading us onward with new incidents or filling in the outlines of what we already know. For *Great Expectations* is an admirable example of one of Lionel Trilling's many dicta about 'Manners, Morals and the Novel': 'The novel, then, is a perpetual quest for reality, the field of its research being always the social world, the material of its analysis being always manners as the indication of the direction of man's soul.'

2. Characterisation

Dickens, like Shakespeare, was a creator as well as an inheritor of the English language and many of the identifiable catch-phrases attached to his characters are known only at one remove from the novels as a phrase or a name. In this merely verbal sense Falstaff and Sarah Gamp, Oliver Twist's request and Malvolio's rebuke, Sidney Carton's dying words and Horatio's epitaph on Hamlet, all share the same kind of immortality. The obvious danger, then, is to allow the expected Dickensian qualities to blind us to the peculiar excellences and restraints of a particular novel, especially in a novel as well organised and as carefully executed as *Great Expectations*. This novel, too, has its catch-phrases and some of its characters are as comically grotesque as any that went before; but they are not exuberantly scattered throughout the story: with few exceptions they are made to serve the novelist's turn with the utmost economy.

Dickens has succeeded in integrating a considerable number of his minor, 'humorous' (in the Jonsonian sense) characters into the main stream of his novel: there are few failures. It is inevitable that Mrs. Joe should give up 'the Rampage' and cease to bring up anyone 'by hand' once she was murderously attacked, but even she continues a vicarious and posthumous existence in the many-sided use made of Pumblechook, who is revived time and time again throughout the story in order to act as a comic claque and to represent that quite common obtuseness of judgement that fails to recognise the change of character that takes place behind too-familiar faces. Trabb's boy is also resurrected for the sake of the story—and perhaps to hint at the unchanging quality of life in the small town—but a newly minted character could have served *his* turn. The soldiers at the beginning of the first Stage, like the Customs Officers and law men at the end of the story, the hangers-on in Little Britain, or the judge and jurors in the Court of Sessions, have the merest walking-on parts necessary for crowd scenes. This is the rôle, too, designed for the toadies at Satis House, for Mr. and Mrs. Hubble, for Mrs. Brandley of Richmond and, one must add regretfully, for Bill Barley and his gentle daughter, Clara.

Once these characters are introduced into the story Dickens seems compelled to bring them to some semblance of life. The *Uncommercial*

Traveller reveals quite plainly that Boz never lost his ear for natural dialogue—whether real or invented—nor his eye for the eccentric touches in scene, dress, figure or situation. In some of his earlier novels situations appear to have been invented in order to display the particular Bozian gifts at the expense of the narrative structure; on such occasions, one's dissatisfaction is not with his vital capacity to bring new characters to life but with his abandonment of them. There is little of this dis-satisfaction in the characters mentioned above: Bill Barley is a welcome relief from the tense and sombre stretches of story that follow Mag-witch's return; the sergeant and his soldiers at the Forge help to fill in time (and delay suspense) as functionally and successfully as the 'grizzled male creature, the "Jack" of the little causeway' does while Magwitch is making his last attempt at escape. Even Pumblechook's nauseating 'May I' strikes an acceptable note of the sycophancy which accompanies all sudden realisations of 'expectations'. But, then, Dickens persevered with Pumblechook and for some unknown reason abandoned Mrs. Belinda Pocket to oblivion after rounding out her snobbish pretensions to quite considerable proportions in one and a half chapters. There is no comparable dismissal in the entire novel.

The next group of characters to be considered are much more closely integrated into the accidental occurences that surround the centrally-placed fable of the rise and fall of Pip's good fortune. They are, in order of appearance—and almost of departure—Wopsle, Compeyson, Orlick, Herbert, Drummle, Startop and Wemmick (carrying with him the Aged Parent and that best of all portable properties, Miss Skiffins). Startop is the odd man out in this group: he is a shadowy creation, a necessary strong arm attached to an ordinary body, who is vital to the action at the climax of the play and, just possibly, a thematic foil to Drummle's pretensions. The other six characters contribute as much to the theme of the novel as they do to the action—if, indeed, the two aspects of the book's central design can be separated. Apart from his identifica-tion of Compeyson in the theatre, Wopsle follows his own fantastic dream of fame as surely as Pip does, but without any final disillusion-ment: his world of fantasy is as thin as the eighteenth-century play's projection of George Barnwell the London apprentice. Compeyson, like Drummle, is essential to the mechanics of the many-tiered plot and also shows up the basic unreality of Magwitch's assumption that 'being a gentleman' (by birth or through unearned wealth) is one of the best blessings he can bestow on the blacksmith's lad. Orlick is a grotesque creation: part ogre, part unrealised demon king from Pantomine, part Cain and, at times, part villain from the cheapest melodrama, he stalks through the marsh country and the dark fastnesses of the urban underworld like Grendel in the Old English poem *Beowulf*. His very name, though copied by Dickens from an authentic list, seems to mark him down for violence, shame and the gallows. He is a Caliban without the poetic speeches. The conception of Wemmick seems to grow under the novelist's pen as the novel proceeds. When he is first described to us (Chapter 21) we immediately recognise the Dickensian play of fancy reserved for a comic figure: 'I found him to be a dry man, rather short in stature, with a square wooden face, whose expression seemed to have been imperfectly chipped out with a dull-edged chisel. . . . His mouth was such a post-office of a mouth that he had a mechanical appearance of smiling . . .'. At Walworth he is fitted into a wooden miniature castle like a child's toy soldier and seems all set to become a necessary toy, a source for Dickens's bizarre image-making and no more. Quickly he is more closely identified with the central action of Provis's return and his function in the novel is enlarged. He plays a variety of parts and sounds many chords in the narrator's recollections. His suburban pastoral existence is manifestly inferior to life at the Forge; his two contrasting natures (at Walworth and Little Britain) are shrewd comments on the nature of work in a growing metropolis; his small-minded, yet realistic attitude to love and portable property is sharply contrasted with Pip's extravagances. He is a courier to Newgate and he supplies some clues to the gaps in the novel's pre-history. And yet so sure is Dickens's touch that despite these multifarious functions he remains throughout as the Wooden Wemmick whom we first meet in Chapter 21. Carlos Lynes (*Forms of Modern Fiction*, p. 185) discusses André Gide's refusal to 'follow through' his characters when they are first introduced to the reader because of his 'unwillingness to compromise the spontaneity of his future response by his present choice'. Dickens knows nothing of this unwillingness: he is quite prepared to allow Wemmick some spontaneous touches of 'human' affection. His cautious arm steals around Miss Skiffins's waist in order to provide touches of humour; his sudden outburst of compassion in Jaggers' office occurs at a critical moment in Pip's desperate search into the origins of Estella. But these are exceptional moments of liberation from the wooden frame inside which Dickens has placed him: he comes 'alive' when it suits the author and not in response to any spontaneous impulse of his own.

Two characters, Molly (housekeeper to Jaggers) and Matthew Pocket (father of Herbert, relative of Miss Havisham and tutor to Pip) are not easily assigned to any category: each plays a minor part in the story, neither is fully-drawn and yet together they add depth to the 'moral fable' that lies barely concealed beneath the tale of Pip's expectations. Neither character is completely visualised for the reader; while Matthew, in particular, could fit smoothly into the world of *Alice in Wonderland*, Molly could slip easily into the nightmare world of *The Woman in White*. The reader's portrait of each character is deduced from what they do (or have done) and not from any visual or verbal qualities which are imposed upon the reader's consciousness by the novelist. Fulfilling necessary rôles in the superficial plot, they are essentially allegorical personages. Matthew stands for many qualities which touch the quick of the moral problems raised by Pip's easy accession to wealth: improvidence, a gentlemanly ideal of education, an old-fashioned conception of honour, impracticability in the conduct of his career or his domestic life, etc. He is a Compeyson who has not gone wrong and for whom nothing has gone right. In contrast to his over-refined and ineffectually educated nature, Molly stands for the intuitive world of instincts and uncontrolled passions. The power of the law and of fear hold the maimed, almost animal-like creature in check; she represents forces inimical to society which might, at any moment, break loose and help to destroy it. Even more obviously than Matthew she belongs to the thematic, subconscious world of the novel; another addition to the crowded gallery of abnormal, maladjusted characters that exerted such a powerful fascination over Dickens's imagination.

All the remaining characters play a major part in the dramatic and thematic world of *Great Expectations*: Joe, Magwitch, Jaggers, Miss Havisham, Estella, Biddy and Herbert. Of these seven, the two last are the least significant: both are firmly embedded in the plot-structure of the narrative and each throws a clear light on the tale's central theme. Together with Estella and Pip they represent the younger generation that is operated upon by the designs, tyrannies and misjudgements of their elders. The essential continuing life of the novel—which moves beyond the terminal dates of the tale precisely because the novel's narrative technique leads one *à la recherche du temps perdu*—rests in their hands; when Miss Havisham has been consumed by fire and Magwitch has failed to survive his baptism in the waters of the Thames, the life of the novel still goes forward. Equally with the other major characters, Biddy and Herbert change under the novelist's hand as the story develops and the original, half-comic, grotesquely conceived plot is transformed into a critique of an acquisitive society. Biddy in the Dame's School is far removed (in conception, presentation and function) from the world of Estella; long before the novel ends she and Estella are presented to the reader, through the eyes and memory of Pip the narrator, as complementary aspects of desirable female nature. In contrast to Pip and Herbert, both young ladies know quite clearly what they wish to get out of life: the final resolution of Pip's love for Estella is supported by his (and our) understanding of Biddy's essentially sane acceptance of her rôle as a wife and mother. In similar fashion, Herbert begins his life as a comic foil to Pip, the blacksmith's boy, before he, too, is involved with, and integrated into, the wider and deeper stretches of the second and third stages of Pip's journey. Born and bred as a gentleman and destined to find happiness and congenial employment through the efforts of others, his function as Pip's *alter ego* is an obvious one. But, like Biddy, he has to stay in the story until the moral plot has been satisfactorily worked out—and Pip has emerged from his dream world—and so, for the present-day reader, he shares in some of the sentimental atmosphere with which Dickens invests the last chapters of the novel. His very last speech in the novel (Chapter 55) gives a clear example of Dickens's power of realising a character's development by means of dialogue:

'And then I shall come back for the dear little thing, and the dear little thing and I will walk quietly into the nearest church. Remember! The blessed darling comes of no family, my dear Handel, and never looked into the red book, and hasn't a notion about her grandpapa. What a fortune for the son of my mother!' (After this moment of critical self-awareness the reference to Herbert at the end of Chapter 58 is quite superfluous, unless it serves to demonstrate Pip's need to tidy up his narrative before the final curtain falls.) Joe, too, has to undergo many chameleon-like changes of character because his original, grotesquely conceived part in the story is affected by the novelist's deepening purpose once the second Stage of Pip's progress is under way. The symbolic function of his character is writ large: like Biddy (and Orlick) he stands for an older, virtuous (or evil) way of life untouched by a society which bases its standards on the possession of unearned wealth. Like them, too, he is conceived in terms of an older stage-convention in which Mr. Wopsle would have felt quite at home. But, under the softening and educative influence of Biddy the gratuitous comic touches —traces of the rather foolish, too good-natured, giant—are erased from his character until only the occasional reversion to dialect and the phrase 'dear old chap' remain. Significantly, too, when Pip has to meet the murderous challenge of Orlick's hatred—a theme that runs right back to the story's beginning—Joe is absent from the marsh-land: Pip has to meet this crisis on his own, unsustained by the antique virtues for which Joe stands, like Adam in *As You Like It*. There is no subtlety in his portrait; his actions never surprise us, not are we sceptical of other people's widely differing reactions to him. His character lives through his speeches which—like those of some Ben Jonson or Sheridan character —are sympathetically conceived. The dialect he speaks is, of course, a stage dialect; we accept its 'genuineness' because we know in our hearts (not in our minds) the special virtues that Joe represents and with which momentarily we are ready to identify ourselves.

The characters of Miss Havisham, and Mr. Jaggers are more complex than this because reader, author and narrator are so entangled in their presentation. On the surface Miss Havisham belongs as much to the world of childhood fable as does Joe or Biddy or Orlick: in the early days of Pip's first Stage she evokes memories of the Snow Maiden and the Witch of Teutonic fairy-tales. For, at this period in his recollections, Pip himself tends to think of various incidents in terms of boyhood fables. When he sets out for London and takes his leave of Miss Havisham (Chapter 19) this childhood vision of his early life is still dominant:

'She looked at Sarah Pocket with triumph in her weird eyes, and so I left my fairy godmother, with both her hands on her crutch stick, standing in the midst of the dimly lighted room beside the rotten bride-cake that was hidden in cobwebs.'

Thereafter Miss Havisham is involved more deeply in the social implications of the moral fable; later still, she is intricately entangled in the recapitulated earlier history of Magwitch, Compeyson and Arthur. Throughout the second Stage of Pip's career she, too, participates in this desperate game of educating a young adolescent for the adult, social world. As this process draws to its close (Chapter 38), in one of the usual set stage-pieces of dialogue which Dickens adopts in order to develop the Estella–Miss Havisham relationship, the fairy godmother discovers that her system of unsentimental education has a cutting side to it. Estella, she finds, can be 'hard and proud' to her benefactress as well as to the rest of mankind. From this moment Dickens alters Miss Havisham's character, while retaining the bizarre setting in which she was initially conceived. During the third Stage the reader not only becomes possessed of all the facts of her pre-history, he is made to feel sympathy and compassion for her desperate attempts to redress ancient wrongs and to cross the boundaries that separate her nightmare world from the common daylight of normal existence.

At first Jaggers emerges from the shadowy background of Satis House as an odd figure with a typical Dickensian gesture by which he can be recognised. He swiftly dominates the second Stage of the novel and, in time, spills over into the novel's pre-history. And yet his character never takes on its own independent life, as Joe's character seems to do whenever Dickens begins to invent dialogue for him to say. In a note on the genesis of *Chance* Conrad writes in these terms about the principal character: 'I simply followed Captain Anthony. Each of us was bent on capturing his own dream.' Jaggers certainly grows in significance as the story progresses. The more we learn about him and his methods the deeper becomes our involvement in the conflict between natural justice and legal administration, and, for added measure, the clearer becomes our understanding of Dickens's constant reference to his accusing finger and his perpetual, Pilate-like washing of his hands. He becomes the receptacle for Dickens's intense feelings about the problem of crime and punishment and the means whereby the author can draw upon his fascinated visual memories of courts, prisons and the underworld. Nor does Dickens miss the opportunity to use this superb performer as the principal character in a series of powerful dramatic scenes. And yet the full potential of this character is never realised within the pages of the novel. Apart from a few touches Jaggers remains a public figure acting out his life in a public capacity: even the motivation of his long domination of Molly is never made explicit from the narrative or expressed in clear terms by either Pip or his creator. In the last resort we realise that Dickens does not rely on character analysis, but on appropriate dialogue and contrived scenes, in order to endow his characters with the verisimilitude of a real existence.

R. W. Stallman (*Forms of Modern Fiction*, p. 234) has elaborately likened the art of fiction to an aquarium and claims that what makes the characters appear as 'life-like' is 'that marvellous liquidity of meaning through which they move'. This is an apt allegory of the kind of life with which Dickens seems to endow Jaggers, Miss Havisham, Joe, Herbert and Biddy once they have been integrated into the rapidly widening world of Pip's second Stage. The remaining characters, Provis and Estella, are so inextricably involved in the central functioning of Pip's recollections and the author's own personal commitment in the situation that he has created, that they cannot be adequately interpreted without the analysis of Pip's dual rôle as actor and narrator of the tale.

3. Pip as Narrator and Protagonist

From the outset Dickens took great care to safeguard *Great Expectations* from the complicated personal involvement which is evident in *David Copperfield* and which, at times, makes the earlier novel such compulsive, magnetic reading. By no stretch of probability can Pip's career be made to run parellel with either that of Dickens or of his forebears. One commentator has made much of Estella's name as a 'lawless anagram' on that of Dickens's mistress, Ellen Lawless Ternan, but even he can make nothing of Magwitch. So successfully has Dickens maintained Pip's fictitious existence that even the moralising comments (or slight touches of a 'layman's religion'), which are present in many of his contributions to *Household Words* and *All The Year Around*, occur infrequently in the course of the novel. Pip believes to some extent in supernatural hints of coming events and he is very sensitive to the promptings of a guilty conscience, but these qualities are consistently portrayed as part of his nature. Similarly, the boy who was only partially cowed by his sister's crude principles of right and wrong and who broke so many rules in order to help the convict on the marsh is still recognisably the young man who decided to seek rough justice for Provis and who refused to believe that the full panoply of English Law had the right to condemn him to death. The warmth of his affections and his basic impulsiveness are clearly portrayed in everything that he does. His devotion to Estella and to Herbert, like his ardent pursuit of the ideal of gentlemanly conduct, form but one side of a coin that matches his other less noble actions: the fierce rejection of Joe in the second Stage, the undisguised repugnance for Provis, the generous self-sacrificing attempt to save Miss Havisham and Magwitch, the visit to the lime-kiln, his instinted admiration for Jaggers's intellect, and even the sudden decision to marry Biddy. Wherever we test it, we find that Pip's character and actions are all of a piece: the character is finely conceived and carefully portrayed with considerable psychological verisimilitude.

There are many moments in the story when the reader dislikes Pip but such moments lie rarely, if ever, outside the novelist's control. Pip is himself his own severe critic and on the whole Dickens has succeeded in saving him from smugness or hypocrisy. Many examples of such

critical moments in the reader-narrator relationship could be brought
forward, but the best proof of Dickens's success in maintaining this
particular knife-edge balance rests on our acceptance of the authenticity
of the entire narrative, from the enlarged over-size world of the young
Pip's memories of the graveyard to the careful understatement of the
final chapter.

Our acceptance of the apparent verisimilitude of the narrative depends
largely upon Dickens's skill in the gradual unfolding and matching of
events so that each revelation, when it occurs, latches on to existing
information that the reader already possesses. The validity of Dickens's
employment of repeated symbols, scenes and incidents depends on our
acceptance of Pip's veracity as an observer which, in its turn, guarantees
the unity of conception of the entire narrative as an exploration through
memory of significant, causally-related events that occurred the day
before yesterday. The careful plotting which marks this tightly constructed narrative creates a suitable, external form for the content of the
tale which is based upon, and closely follows, a middle-aged man's
probings into the formative years of his life. As the narrative progresses
forward in time, the interrelatedness of events and principal characters
is extended backwards into the novel's pre-history, until all the relevant
facts are laid bare and a clear-eyed but chastened Pip is linked to a subdued and softened Estella at a place which is close to the story's origins.

This circular plot-movement is closely paralleled by Pip's relationships
with two other principal characters, Magwitch and Estella. Magwitch's
picaro nature and false notions of gentility are reflected in Pip's own
life; each shows a capacity for sustained and self-sacrificing devotion to
another person and, at the end of Magwitch's life, Pip seems to mingle
his passion for Estella with his frenetic devotion to her father. The
grotesque tragi-comic conception with which Dickens began the story
is never completely abandoned, for, although it is difficult to swallow
within the context of the novel, the reader is expected to accept Estella
as the child of Magwitch and Molly. The more one reflects on this
relationship (and the final assumption that Estella marries Pip, the
narrator) the more difficult it becomes to accept Pip's story as essentially
a clearly-defined attack on a whole society and the more powerful do
the picaresque and fairy-tale aspects of the story appear to be. For the
purposes of the tale Magwitch, Estella and Pip are rootless in origins,
unlocated in society and free from obligations to the ordinary claims of

the average citizen. The relationship of Magwitch and Estella to other characters in the story is predatory and (in their different ways) destructive; the positive aspects of their nature are preserved only in Pip's memory of their conversations and acts with him. Even the final meeting between Pip and Estella is occasioned by their joint acts of memory, 'realised' in a place, rather than by any willed desire to find each other and so establish a new fruitful relationship. In Pip's eyes all three of them have expiated their past crimes independently and when he and Estella leave the ruined garden a chapter in their lives has been irrevocably and finally closed.

Conceived as outsiders, Magwitch and Estella still react violently against the other characters and against the ordinary conventions of 'society', in so far as that term can be used for the loosely-connected locations in which Pip's story is enacted. Magwitch is classless, almost codeless, and a creature of instinctive obsessions; he has all the marks of a frontiersman who is at home only in the open air. Australia, with its wide spaces (and its solitude), is the ideal place for him to make a fortune. And yet he is impelled to return to, and to clash with, an older society which has rejected him from childhood. He is the touchstone by which all the false notions of gentility and breeding are tested and found wanting and, ultimately, his devotion to Pip's memory—the sole positive virtue in his make-up—brings about Pip's own regeneration. Magwitch's narrative of his life's story is one of Dickens's supreme strokes of artistry: it pulls together many hidden threads of narrative and, at the same time, acts as a testimony in justification of his conduct. Thereafter Magwitch's biography dominates the novel's social content like a jagged rocky outcrop above fields of corn: the eye is forcibly drawn back to it in wonder and enquiry. Estella, too, possesses the same catalytic quality. Apart from her rôle as Pip's adored one—the one spark of self-effacement in his middle stage of development—her principal function in the novel is to pour doubt on the excessive feelings of those who surround her and to stand for those principles of passionless reason (based on self-interest and twisted ideals) which, Dickens seems to suggest, lie at the heart of a genteel, acquisitive society. She operates in the private world of the affections while her father's conduct provokes conflict with the public claims of society. Conceived in obscurity, concealed as an infant, educated in the twilight world of Satis House and brought to maturity in the social night life of the fashionable world, she is gentle only with

Pip (travelling on the open road) and expresses her own sense of inade-quate development (in Chapter 38) as part of her inability 'to take naturally to the daylight'. Like Miss Havisham, Estella seems to lack an independent existence of her own, until disaster claims her and bitter experience softens her nature. For Dickens's powerful, grotesque por-trait of Satis House and its inhabitants has been too successfully executed. Despite the admirable exchanges of dialogue there between Pip, Miss Havisham, Jaggers and Estella, those sections of the novel that are located within its walls remain stage scenes redolent of melodrama and pantomime. Even Estella's one firm link with society—her marriage to Drummle—is tinged with farce because he is no more than a flat, pasteboard character: there are countless characters like him in Restora-tion and eighteenth-century comedy, with a label, 'Upper-Class Booby', around his neck and with no independent realisation in terms of action or dialogue. Unlike Magwitch, Estella is never completely integrated into the social theme which Dickens developed out of and around the Never-Never Land of Pip's first Stage of life.

Both Estella and her father are indissolubly linked with Pip's own recollected life: they draw much of their vitality directly from his peculiarly personal vision of, and judgement upon, the kind of life they have been compelled to live by the pressure of external circumstances. Pip's desperate, self-punishing search for Estella's true antecedents is presented to the reader in stronger terms and with more cogency than the effect of that discovery upon the future course of events can warrant. The discovery does not help Magwitch—even his recognition of the fact is uncertain; the status of Molly is never raised once the answer has been found, and Estella is never informed of the fact. Why is this? What purpose does this particular line of enquiry serve in the carefully formulated construction of the novel? Possibly, this search for Estella's ancestry could be interpreted as an unconscious blunder on Dickens's part. He sedulously shielded his children and his friends from any knowledge of the black (ungenteel?) spots in his own education and childhood training. There is some mystification in the close parallels that exist between parts of *David Copperfield* and his own unpublished autobiographical fragment. He has left on record a bitter denunciation of his parent's neglect of his formal education. Are we not justified in assuming that, because *Great Expectations* is shaped from some of the more sensitive spots in Dickens's own childhood memories, he would at times be unable to control his pen and would explore imaginatively certain suppressed areas of his own life, even if such exploration was irrelevant to Pip's story? I think this is a mistaken view of the novel. Naturally, Dickens drew on his own childhood recollections for much of the detail of Pip's childhood, grotesque though it is, and, to this extent, Pip sees and hears the world through Dickens's own senses. But Pip cannot be confused with Dickens and Dickens has taken great pains to keep their identities apart. The carefully interwoven plot construction, the repeated themes, symbols and images, the studied care taken over details of time and place, all show Dickens's determination to 'distance' Pip's narrative and so to separate Pip's life story from his own. The author of *Great Expectations* was a wealthy man, assured of his place in society, with distinct and vocal opinions on social and moral questions and, above all, with a shrewd capacity for exploiting an acquisitive society for his own profit. Pip's ineptitude is made acceptable to us, not because of his failure to achieve great material expectations, but because we are made to share his search for personal identity. His tortured self-questionings and periodic moments of severe self-examination are part of his nature; we quickly learn to accept them as his own without attributing them to the author. They are no more out of place here than are those of Christian in *Pilgrim's Progress*, and for the same reason: they objectify preoccupations shared at some time by all human beings. Pip's ultimate standards of moral judgement are vitiated by the intellectual weakness of theological debate in Victorian England, but nothing can dim one's admiration for his single-minded pursuit of the truth as he sees it. The search for Estella's identity forms part of this pursuit and is complementary to the constant enquiry into the springs of his own conduct throughout all the actions that follow upon that first casual encounter in the graveyard. As Pip ponders the life story of Magwitch and Estella, in order to shape his narrative, he finds reasons and excuses for *their* conduct too; and, as the narrative grows, all the other characters are subjected to the same critical scrutiny. In the process the functions of the acceptable social code, of the rule of law, of the claims of religion, of education, of the family, and of the sources of wealth are involved in Pip's obstinate questionings and are subordinated to his ultimate demand for personal fulfilment through the provision of opportunities for acceptable employment (outside England) and domestic happiness. 'The bitterness of Dickens's exposure of Pip's parasitism' (G. B. Shaw) is followed by a modified happiness which is based on a reconciliation to the claims of society and of other individuals upon him.

A. O. J. Cockshut detects a faltering in the 'devastating satirical demands' of the story and suggests that *Great Expectations* reveals 'a new timidity' in Dickens's critique of Victorian England. Such a conclusion ignores the novelist's careful attempts to keep the narrative within the fallible bounds of Pip's memory which, in the event, attracts to itself those incidents and events that are most deeply involved with Pip's own personal history. As the threads of the narrative are pulled together the reader senses some of that artificial telescoping of events which is common to most of Dickens's novels, except that in *Great Expectations* this matters less and arouses fewer question marks than the end of *David Copperfield*. The novel turns naturally and inevitably upon itself and we are left to assume that the orphan child, who began his tale with a backward look and some uncertainty about his own name, has at last found a companion and some modified assurance upon which to build his future expectations. The fairy-tale that developed into an allegory has at last become an ordinary, human pilgrimage.

4. Style

During the last two decades interpreters of Dickens's novels have paid an inordinate amount of attention to the social implications of his novels, to their relationship to Victorian society and to the symbols and themes that lie hidden like reefs just beneath the surface of his rapidly moving narrative. As a result of this concentration of interest on the sociological and, indeed, psychological implications of his novels—particularly the later ones—less close attention has been given to the quality of Dickens's style. For this reason alone this chapter will contain typical examples of the many different kinds of writing in this one novel in order to suggest that the chameleon-like quality of Dickens's style in *Great Expectations* is part of the novel's strength, and, at the same time, contains clear evidence of the novel's weaknesses. In *David Copperfield* there is a great deal of compulsive writing: one feels that the narrator is pouring out his heart and for long stretches of the novel one is unable to put it down, so intense is the urgency of the narrator's tone. *Great Expectations* is written in a much more 'distanced' manner: Dickens allows Pip to relate incidents and events which are similar to sensitive spots in the novelist's own life without becoming too deeply involved himself in the narration. Mr. T. S. Eliot's dictum, that 'the more perfect the artist, the more completely separate in him will be the man who suffers and the mind which creates', expresses succinctly my considered opinion of Dickens's aim—if not his final achievement—in this second attempt at an imaginative re-creation of the 'twice told tales of infancy'.

George Orwell's opinion that Dickens's fertility of invention consists 'not so much of characters and situations, as of turns of phrase and concrete details' is echoed by most critics. Shaw learned from Dickens 'that it is possible to combine a mirror-like exactness of character drawing with the wildest extravagances of humorous expression'; H. Blair Rouse praises Dickens because he adapted his reporter's gifts to express a 'sense of history in physical action and surface portrayals'; John H. Hagan believes that in order to give his theme 'imaginative embodiment' Dickens is constantly bringing concrete images from the marsh-land, the mud and the hulks into the apparently tranquil indoor life of the novel.

At all times Dickens is in control of his gift for intense visual recall. The following passage (from Chapter 40) shows his ability to use the observation of details in order to convey Pip's shrinking from Provis:

'The influences of his solitary hut-life were upon him besides, and gave him a savage air that no dress could tame; added to these were the influences of his subsequent branded life among men, and crowning all, his consciousness that he was dodging and hiding now. In all his ways of sitting and standing, and eating and drinking—of brooding about, in a high-shouldered reluctant style—of taking out his great horn-handled jackknife and wiping it on his legs and cutting his food—of lifting light glasses and cups to his lips, as if they were clumsy pannikins—of chopping a wedge off his bread, and soaking up with it the last fragments of gravy round and round his plate, as if to make the most of an allowance, and then drying his fingers on it, and then swallowing it—in these ways and in a thousand other small nameless instances arising every minute in the day, there was Prisoner, Felon, Bondsman, plain as plain could be.'

In contrast to these staccato phrases the following rhetorical account of Pip's delirium (Chapter 57) seems to convey the wandering movement of the patient:

'That I had a fever and was avoided, that I suffered greatly, that I often lost my reason, that the time seemed interminable, that I confounded impossible existences with my own identity; that I was a brick in the house wall, and yet entreating to be released from the giddy place where the builders had set me; that I was a steel beam of a vast engine, clashing and whirling over a gulf, and yet that I implored in my own person to have the engine stopped, and my part in it hammered off; that I passed through these phases of disease, I know of my own remembrance, and did in some sort know at the time. That I sometimes struggled with real people, in the belief that they were murderers, and that I would all at once comprehend that they meant to do me good, and would then sink exhausted in their arms, and suffer them to lay me down, I also knew at the time. But, above all, I knew that there was a constant tendency in all these people—who, when I was very ill, would present all kinds of extraordinary transformations of the human face, and would be much dilated in size—above all, I say, I knew that there was an extraordinary tendency in all these people, sooner or later, to settle down into the likeness of Joe.'

Great Expectations was carefully designed in three emergent stages that assist the reader to share Pip's ever-deepening probes into the suppressed layers of recollection. The simplicity of the relation of childhood memories in Stage One is reflected in a general directness of style: the texture of Stage Three is much more complex, for, as the action speeds up, it is accompanied by substantial revelations about the pre-history of Magwitch, Compeyson, Miss Havisham and Estella, which are reflected in more frequent echoes of images and scenes from the two earlier stages. Graham Greene believes that this novel was written in 'delicate and exact poetic cadences, the music of memory, that so influenced Proust'. The two extracts that follow (the first from Chapter 48 and the second from Chapter 58) show the consistency with which Dickens used this device of recall in order to create two quite distinct moods:

'He dismissed her, and she glided out of the room. But she remained before me, as plainly as if she were still there. I looked at those hands, I looked at those eyes, I looked at that flowing hair; and I compared them with other hands, other eyes, other hair, that I knew of, and with what those might be after twenty years of a brutal husband and a stormy life. I looked again at those hands and eyes of the housekeeper, and thought of the inexplicable feeling that had come over me when I last walked—not alone—in the ruined garden, and through the deserted brewery. I thought how the same feeling had come back when I saw a face looking at me, and a hand waving to me, from a stage-coach window; and how it had come back again and had flashed about me like lightning, when I had passed in a carriage—not alone—through a sudden glare of light in a dark street. I thought how one link of association had helped that identification in the theatre, and how such a link, wanting before, had been riveted for me now, when I had passed by a chance swift from Estella's name to the fingers with their knitting action, and the attentive eyes. And I felt absolutely certain that this woman was Estella's mother.'

'The June weather was delicious. The sky was blue, the larks were soaring high over the green corn, I thought all that country-side more beautiful and peaceful by far than I had ever known it to be yet. Many pleasant pictures of the life that I would lead there, and of the change for the better that would come over my character when I had a guiding spirit at my side whose simple faith and clear home-wisdom I had proved, beguiled my way. They awakened a tender emotion in me; for my heart was softened by my return, and such a change had come to pass, that I felt like one who was toiling home barefoot from distant travel, and whose wanderings had lasted many years.

'The schoolhouse where Biddy was mistress, I had never seen; but the little roundabout lane, by which I entered the village for quietness' sake, took me past it. I was disappointed to find that the day was a holiday; no children were there, and Biddy's house was closed. Some hopeful notion of seeing her, busily engaged in her daily duties, before she saw me, had been in my mind and was defeated.

'But the forge was a very short distance off, and I went towards it under the sweet green limes, listening for the clink of Joe's hammer. Long after I ought to have heard it, and long after I had fancied I heard it and found it but a fancy, all was still. The limes were there, and the white thorns were there, and the chestnut-trees were there, and their leaves rustled harmoniously when I stopped to listen; but the clink of Joe's hammer was not in the midsummer wind.

'Almost fearing, without knowing why, to come in view of the forge, I saw it at last, and saw it was closed. No gleam of fire, no glittering shower of sparks, no roar of bellows; all shut up, and still.'

The kinds of narrative prose given above form a considerable part of the staple style of the novel; but, although Dickens takes considerable pains to remind the reader that it is Pip's eye that has seen these things, Pip's memory that recalls them, and Pip's voice that gives them expression, he also relies heavily on reported dialogue in order to support Pip's memories with the suggestion that it depends scrupulously on fact. Walter C. Phillips (*Dickens, Reade, and Collins, Sensation Novelists*, p. 219) has argued that *Great Expectations*, like the work of Reade and Collins, is a significant milestone in the progress from the long, discursive three-decker novel to the later one-volume story: there was among these novelists (grouped around Dickens) a pronounced taste for villainy, violence, and crime, but they adopted a refinement of method which included a 'mode of expression that is necessary for a play'. They liked to call their works dramatic novels. Dickens had always relied on invented, fantastic dialogue as a foil to his vividly reported, descriptive scenes; in his mature novels he came to rely heavily on the use of appropriate dialogue. *Great Expectations* is rich in illustrations of his gift for reported speech that is at once 'realistic' and dramatic. Miss Havisham would never have left her fairy-tale attic but for her later verbal exchanges with Estella and Pip; Jaggers lives for us largely through his words; Joe's own fantastic brand of English endears him to us much more than the incidents which describe him as the soft-hearted giant. Chapter 22, with the long conversation between Pip and Herbert about the latter's expectations, is a good example of Dickens's ability to adapt ordinary conversation to the advancement of his story and to our knowledge of its characters. The long undulating exchange between Jaggers and Pip in Chapter 40 (about Provis—'in New South Wales') shows Dickens's constant determination, and ability, to relieve moments of tension in the plot by a series of theatrical interchanges. (Is this fixed determination of the novelist to enliven the more sombre parts of Pip's memories the reason for A. O. J. Cockshut's opinion that, because the theme is 'deadly serious', the 'tone is too jolly'?) There is always, of course, the danger that the novelist's dialogue becomes too literary for all dramatic purposes: a danger that is always present in the later stages of the novel when Estella is the object of memory. This passage, for example, from Chapter 44 can belong only to the author, who quickly makes Pip call it a 'rhapsody':

' "Out of my thoughts! You are part of my existence, part of myself. You have been in every line I have ever read, since I first came here, the rough common boy whose poor heart you wounded even then. You have been in every prospect I have ever seen since—on the river, on the sails of the ships, on the marshes, in the clouds, in the light, in the darkness, in the wind, in the woods, in the sea, in the streets. You have been the embodiment of every graceful fancy that my mind has ever become acquainted with. The stones of which the strongest London buildings are made, are not more real, or more impossible to be displaced by your hands, than your presence and influence have been to me, there and everywhere, and will be. Estella, to the last hour of my life, you cannot choose but remain part of my character, part of the little good in me, part of the evil. But, in this separation I associate you only with the good, and I will faithfully hold you to that always, for you must have done me far more good than harm, let me feel now what sharp distress I may. O God bless you, God forgive you!" '

As Pip's rhapsody suggests, the oft-repeated charge against Dickens's sentimentalism can be brought against some of the writing in *Great Expectations*. Generally such passages jar on the modern reader and, after every allowance has been made for Victorian taste, one regrets that Dickens wrote them. A defence of some of them could be made because the novel is itself an account of a 'sentimental education' that leads to Pip's greater self-awareness; however, it is well to note, first, that the moments of sentimentalism are clustered around certain characters only and, secondly, that Dickens was capable of breaking the sentimental mood at will. Estella, naturally, attracts to herself all Pip's desire to dwell longingly over the past. The following extract (from Chapter 33) illustrates admirably how a passage that begins with firmness of tone can suddenly degenerate into sentimental observation:

'We came to Richmond all too soon, and our destination there was a house by the Green: a staid old house, where hoops and powder and patches, embroidered coats, rolled stockings, ruffles, and swords, had had their court days many a time. Some ancient trees before the house were still cut into fashions as formal and unnatural as the hoops and wigs and stiff skirts; but their own allotted places in the great procession of the dead were not far off, and they would soon drop into them and go the silent way of the rest.

'A bell with an old voice—which I dare say in its time had often said to the house, Here is the green farthingale, Here is the diamond-hilted sword, Here are the shoes with red heels and the blue solitaire,—sounded gravely in the moonlight, and two cherry-coloured maids came flutter-ing out to receive Estella. The doorway soon absorbed her boxes, and she gave me her hand and a smile, and said good night, and was absorbed likewise. And still I stood looking at the house, thinking how happy I should be if I lived there with her, and knowing that I never was happy with her, but always miserable.

'I got into the carriage to be taken back to Hammersmith, and I got in with a bad heart-ache, and I got out with a worse heart-ache. At our own door I found little Jane Pocket coming home from a little party, escorted by her little lover; and I envied her little lover, in spite of his being subject to Flopson.'

Dickens has a much firmer grip on Pip's betrayal of his feelings for Joe. (Biddy is quite a different proposition!) Chapter 57 provides many examples of Dickens's power to walk the knife-edge between senti-mental gush and the conveying of tenderness in human relationships. Joe's special brand of humorous dialogue, however stagey in origin, is the means by which Dickens contrives to keep his balance:

'For the tenderness of Joe was so beautifully proportioned to my need, that I was like a child in his hands. He would sit and talk to me in the old confidence, and with the old simplicity, and in the old un-assertive protecting way, so that I would half believe that all my life since the days of the old kitchen was one of the mental troubles of the fever that was gone. He did everything for me except the household work, for which he had engaged a very decent woman, after paying off the laundress on his first arrival. " Which I do assure you, Pip," he would often say, in explanation of that liberty; "I found her a tapping the spare bed, like a cask of beer, and drawing off the feathers in a bucket, for sale. Which she would have tapped yourn next, and draw'd it off with you a laying on it, and was then a carrying away the coals gradiw-ally in the soup-tureen and wegetable dishes, and the wine and spirits in your Wellington boots." '

A similar dexterity in the use of verbal humour (and grotesque visual-isation) as a secure bridge across the cosy domestic tears of much Victor-ian literature is shown superbly in the description of Mrs. Joe's funeral (in Chapter 35). Sentiment and *pietas* is never outraged, but the phoney quality of the set funeral is acidly and humorously summed up in Mr. Trabb's businesslike injunction—' "Pocket-handkerchiefs out! We are ready!" ' There can be no ready-made charge of sentimentalism against Dickens when such passages are read carefully. Conrad's preface to *The Nigger of the Narcissus*—a similar act of fictional exploration of autobiographical memories is, perhaps, a safe guide to this problem of how to give due place to the emotions in a novel:—'The changing wisdom of successive generations discards ideas, questions, facts, demolishes theories. But the artist appeals to that part of our being which is not dependent on wisdom; to that in us which is a gift and not an acquisition—and, therefore, more permanently enduring. He speaks to our capacity for delight and wonder, to the sense of mystery surround-ing our lives; to our sense of pity, and beauty, and pain; to the latent feeling of fellowship with all creation—and to the subtle but invincible conviction of solidarity that knits together the loneliness of innumerable hearts, to the solidarity in dreams, in joy, in sorrow, in aspirations, in illusions, in hope, in fear, which binds men to each other, which binds together all humanity—the dead to the living and the living to the unborn.'

If the question of Dickens's sentimentality is a thorny one, the discussion of his humour is a thicket, almost impenetrable to contemporary critics, particularly in analyses of his later works. Dickens was not wedded indissolubly to his comic Muse. Professors Butt and Tillotson (*Dickens at Work*, p. 22) have noted that when Dickens had written too much for any serial number he 'was accustomed to make his cuts at the expense of the comedy'. Dickens, one must assume on the evidence of his periodical writing, never lost the gift for comic invention of dialogue or for the grotesque embroidery and exaggeration of incidents encountered in his constant journeyings and restless walks. I agree with Edgar Johnson (*Charles Dickens: His Tragedy and Triumph*, p. 993) that *Great Expectations* is 'not a melancholy book' in its pervading atmosphere and that 'these joyous moments do not undermine the predominant serious-ness . . . of its theme'. Since it is part of the author's intention that Pip's narrative should catch up within itself half a lifetime's recollections, the novel must of necessity contain many kinds of humour. The exagger-ated, over-serious childhood memories of the adult world, the vividly etched adolescent memories of Satis House, the uncomfortable and irritating memories of Trabb's boy, the patronisingly recalled stages in Mr. Wopsle's histrionic decline and fall, the benevolence that surrounds all the oddities of Wemmick's fantastic life, and the affectionate yet whimsical portrayal of Herbert as a boy, a young man and a business-man—these are staple elements in the texture of Pip's mind as well as in the unfolding events of his life. Other incidents are clearly brought for-ward by the author for our extraneous enjoyment: the young men at Finches Grove, Mrs. Joe on the Rampage, Pumblechook at all times, Mr. and Mrs. Matthew Pocket at home, and Pip and Drummle before the inn fire, are some examples of Dickens's fine sense of the entertain-ment expected of Boz by the reading public.

The comic style is varied and it can become mannered and fall into a reliance on verbal tricks:

'And here I may remark that when Mr. Wopsle referred to me, he considered it a necessary part of such reference to rumple my hair and poke it into my eyes. I cannot conceive why everybody of his standing who visited at our house should always have put me through the same inflammatory process under similar circumstances. Yet I do not call to mind that I was ever in my earlier youth the subject of remark in our social family circle, but some large-handed person took some such ophthalmic steps to patronise me' (Chapter 10).

D

Such a drop in the tension of the writing is frequent in the first stage of Pip's tale and is never quite absent from the entire treatment of Wemmick. Even so, the facetiousness of the following account of his marriage (Chapter 55) is so rare in the third Stage that one suspects Dickens of a desire to send Wemmick out of the story with a boisterous slap of warm-hearted gratitude:

' "Halloa!" said Wemmick. "Here's Miss Skiffins! Let's have a wedding."

'That discreet damsel was attired as usual, except that she was now engaged in substituting for her green kid gloves, a pair of white. The Aged was likewise occupied in preparing a similar sacrifice for the altar of Hymen. The old gentleman, however, experienced so much difficulty in getting his gloves on, that Wemmick found it necessary to put him with his back against a pillar, and then to get behind the pillar himself and pull away at them, while I for my part held the old gentleman round the waist, that he might present an equal and safe resistance. By dint of this ingenious scheme, his gloves were got on to perfection.

'The clerk and clergyman then appearing, we were ranged in order at those fatal rails. True to his notion of seeming to do it all without preparation, I heard Wemmick say to himself as he took something out of his waistcoat-pocket before the service began, "Halloa! Here's a ring!" '

To discount the author's insistence on retaining this tone of good-humoured recollection and to concentrate one's critical attention too closely on the interwoven memories of mist, marsh-land, dark water, mud and prison stench could lead the reader to a lop-sided understanding of Pip's own character and philosophy of life.

Naturally a novel of this length has its passages of tired writing. The indeterminate movement of the following passage (Chapter 16)—quite typical of many of Pip's attempts to come to terms with his sense of guilt—cannot be blamed entirely upon the tone of Lillo's *George Barnwell*:

'It was horrible to think that I had provided the weapon, however undesignedly, but I could hardly think otherwise. I suffered unspeakable trouble while I considered and reconsidered whether I should at last dissolve that spell of my childhood and tell Joe all the story. For months afterwards, I every day settled the question finally in the negative, and reopened and reargued it next morning. The contention came, after all, to this;—the secret was such an old one now, had so grown into me and become a part of myself, that I could not tear it away. In addition to the dread that, having led up to so much mischief, it would be now more likely than ever to alienate Joe from me if he believed it, I had a further restraining dread that he would not believe it, but would assert it with the fabulous dogs and veal-cutlets as a monstrous invention. However, I temporised with myself, of course—for was I not wavering between right and wrong, when the thing is always done?—and resolved to make a full disclosure if I should see any such new occasion as a new chance of helping in the discovery of the assailant.' (A similar inability to give satisfactory expression to the vague promptings of the subconscious mind can be found at the end of Chapter 32.)

At times, too, Dickens's strongly developed visual sense comes between him and the reader. He overdoes the sensational aspect of Orlick's attempt on Pip's life or the fantastic upstairs life of Bill Barley without adding to the pace of the narrative or to our understanding of these minor characters. On the whole Chapter 54 is an exciting and remarkably consistent piece of writing, but even here the visual details can get in the way and, as a consequence, the style flags:

'Our oarsmen were so fresh, by dint of having occasionally let her drive with the tide for a minute or two, that a quarter of an hour's rest proved full as much as they wanted. We got ashore among some slippery stones while we ate and drank what we had with us, and looked about. It was like my own marsh country, flat and monotonous, and with a dim horizon; while the winding river turned and turned, and the great floating buoys upon it turned and turned, and everything else seemed stranded and still. For now the last of the fleet of ships was round the last low point we had headed; and the last green barge, straw-laden, with a brown sail, had followed; and some ballast-lighters, shaped like a child's first rude imitation of a boat, lay low in the mud; and a little squat shoal-lighthouse on open piles, stood crippled in the mud on stilts and crutches; and slimy stakes stuck out of the mud, and slimy stones stuck out of the mud, and red landmarks and tidemarks stuck out of the mud, and an old landing-stage and an old roofless building slipped into the mud, and all about us was stagnation and mud.'

The most notorious example of Dickens's 'set-piece style' is the frequently quoted end of Chapter 38:

'And now that I have given the one chapter to the theme that so filled my heart, and so often made it ache and ache again, I pass on, unhindered, to the event that had impended over me longer yet; the event that had begun to be prepared for, before I knew that the world held Estella, and in the days when her baby intelligence was receiving its first distortions from Miss Havisham's wasting hands.

'In the Eastern story, the heavy slab that was to fall on the bed of state in the flush of conquest was slowly wrought out of the quarry, the tunnel for the rope to hold it in its place was slowly carried through the leagues of rock, the slab was slowly raised and fitted in the roof, the rope was rove to it and slowly taken through the miles of hollow to the great iron ring. All being made ready with much labour, and the hour come, the sultan was aroused in the dead of the night, and the sharpened axe that was to sever the rope from the great iron ring was put into his hand, and he struck with it, and the rope parted and rushed away, and the ceiling fell. So in my case; all the work, near and afar, that tended to the end, had been accomplished; and in an instant the blow was struck, and the roof of my stronghold dropped upon me.'

The tone even of this passage, with its air of apparent detachment and its obvious direct address to the reader, is a rare one in the novel. For it is rather wild to discuss the 'style' of *Great Expectations* as one would discuss the style of Conrad or James Joyce. Apart from the more obvious characteristics of Dickens's gifts as a writer—his eye for significant detail, his ear for comic utterance, his assured command of all the oratorical tricks directed at a known audience—there is a sense in which, in his novels, Dickens had no recognisable 'style' at all. (His periodical style of writing is much more uniform in texture, tone and cadence.) He possessed in abundance a vital energy which enabled him to carry his story forward and the reader with it. Some of his worst excesses derive from his acute awareness of the waiting audience; his excellences, too, depend upon his determination to satisfy that audience's demand for a story. His superb self-assurance does the rest.

5. Themes and Symbols

Recent critics like Edmund Wilson, Lionel Trilling, Edgar Johnson, David Daiches, Monroe Engel, John H. Hagan, John H. Raleigh, Graham Greene and A. O. J. Cockshut have helped to uncover many of the themes and symbols that are embodied in the narrative of Pip's quest for self-fulfilment. To write down a catalogue of all the themes that emerge, in moments of reflection after successive readings of the novel, is to create scepticism about a pre-emptive claim for any single theme as the sole key to the labyrinth of the story's meaning. The list seems endless: crime and punishment; natural justice and the law; pre-destination and free will; the outcast and society; the dignity of labour in an acquisitive society; private lives and public pretensions; the relationship between the instincts and the affections; the operation of time in events and in the subconscious mind; the idea of consequences from one generation to the next; the rôle of education in one's progress towards clear self-awareness; private belief and public profession; the sharp juxtaposition of appearance and reality; violence as a counterpart of 'gentility'. This is by no means an exhaustive list of the clear, intellectual concepts that are woven into the tapestry of the narrative and it takes no account of the multiple symbols that Dickens draws upon in the act of writing in order to keep alive the reader's awareness of his themes while the story of Pip's life is being re-enacted before his eyes: the prison hulks and the marsh, the mists of the flat country being incorporated into the shadows of town life, the open-air freedom of the criminals impinging upon the domestic comfort of his families, the frequent use of the four elements at crucial points in the narrative, Estella's plea for daylight as a counterforce to Satis House and all it stands for, the theatricality of church and Courts of Justice, the deserted garden, and the open sea. Once more the list is longer and more overwhelming than any single solution that can be offered as a clue to the novelist's artistic purpose once Dickens had decided to develop his initial 'grotesque tragi-comic conception' along lines that were parallel to, but not contiguous with, the autobiographical success-story of *David Copperfield*. (For Pip, unlike David, decides to recount his life-story when material prosperity and worldly success have escaped him.) The compilation of these catalogues serves a double purpose: it suggests why some writers are tempted to make exaggerated claims for Dickens's universality as though he were a prose Shakespeare, and it focusses the reader's attention on Dickens's ability so to enmesh the selected incidents from his hero's life in the claims of society and the velleities in the operation of the individual will that the ground plot appears to become a moral fable. 'To know a story when we see one, to know it for a story, to know that it is not reality itself but that it has clear and effective relations with reality—this is one of the great disciplines of the mind.' Of course, Lionel Trilling's apotheosis of the ideal novel is not true at all points for *Great Expectations*—chiefly, I suggest, because while Dickens nearly succeeded in identifying himself with Pip, he retained the right to embroider Pip's narrative with direct addresses to his own beloved' readers; but it does indicate the kind of success that is achieved in this novel when the reader's imagination is caught and held by the rapid unfolding of the tale.

Dickens's device of a three-part structure has helped him to strip his theme to its intellectual essentials without constricting the free flow of its social and psychological implications. Since the entire artifice is based on Pip's conscious act of memory, and since any act of memory is essentially an exploration of events bounded by causation in time and place, Dickens invests each of the three stages with clear-cut, easily grasped temporal and spatial characteristics. Stage One, acted against the marsh-land, the Forge, the inn, the small town and Satis House, is played out against a clearly defined backcloth at a leisurely pace so that unusual incidents are magnified to occupy a dominant significance in Pip's recall of selected childhood events. Stage Two is set against the metropolitan labyrinth of London—pinpointed for us by excursions away from it—where space is so extensive that time, too, seems limitless. At this stage in their emergence from the chrysalis of formative influences, Pip and Estella are allowed to live carelessly and irresponsibly as though freed from all outside obligations and impelled only by the inner need to find personal fulfilment. Inevitably this illusion of freedom is shattered in Stage Three when the claims of the hidden past reach out and shatter their present dreams (and future actions): the cosy, static world of Stage One and the factitious stage-set interiors of Stage Two are thrown rapidly and disjunctively against public events, natural phenomena, and the open ways of the world on land and sea. The

Thames suddenly becomes the gateway to a wider world; Satis House is destroyed; the Forge becomes a genuine family home; the escaped convict dies at peace in a prison hospital. The reverberations, echoes and chain-reactions of these events are certainly brought to a hurried conclusion as the novel ends, but Dickens's instinct is sound when he shuffles his principal subordinate actors off the stage and quickly leads the reader back to the point of rest (in time and place) where the story began. The final marriage of Pip and Estella (the daughter of Magwitch) is fittingly the central dynamic moment from which the whole act of recollection derives its original impulse.

The novel's end, one may argue, is its true beginning: 'I took her hand in mine, and we went out of the ruined place; and, as the morning mists had risen long ago when I first left the forge, so, the evening mists were rising now, and in all the broad expanse of tranquil light they showed to me, I saw no shadow of another parting from her.' Despite the softening (and sentimentalising?) influence of the mist-image, this sentence, like the rest of this much-disputed, altered ending to *Great Expectations*, is not a betrayal of the story that precedes it. For even in this last chapter the offending mist-image serves many purposes. When Pip enters the ruin 'A cold silvery mist had veiled the afternoon'; when he met Estella and saw 'the saddened softened light of the once proud eyes' and the moon began to rise, Pip was reminded of Magwitch's death ('I thought of the placid look at the white ceiling, which had passed away'.) 'The silvery mist' was then touched for the first time 'with the first rays of moonlight'. The conversation that follows is about practical matters which are still relevant to the theme of *Great Expectations*. At last Estella is selling the ground so that homes can be built on the site of Satis House, while Pip who had been educated to expect an empty, parasitic life of obedience to vague, gentlemanly ideals of good form—those ideals of Matthew Pocket, the Finches or Drummle —confesses, 'I work pretty hard for a sufficient living, and therefore— Yes, I do well!' The restrained and sober confession of love that follows and leads into the mellowed wistfulness of Dickens's last paragraph cannot therefore be interpreted as a weak escape from that sombre indictment of an acquisitive society which has formed the back-bone of the novel's seriousness. That theme is still vibrant as the novel ends. Without a doubt the story displays a restricting contraction of interest once Magwitch has died and Pip falls into delirium, but the story would have been incomplete if Pip's own voyage of self-discovery—couched in terms of a regression to childhood scenes and adolescent fantasies— had not been carried through in terms of narrative and dialogue. Modern taste may recoil from the self-revelatory exchanges between Joe, Biddy and Pip while it accepts gratefully the ironic treatment of Pumblechook, the windy donkey's hypocrisy. (Personally I don't think that Dickens was being 'unrealistic' when he made his characters speak from the heart: my own memory of Victorian great-aunts confirms the accuracy of this reporting of sober country folk with strong Evangelical beliefs.) Pip's narrative would have been incomplete and his need for expiation—the driving force behind his narrative—would have remained unfulfilled if Dickens had not matched the exposure of a false money-centred society with a similar exposure of Pip's and Estella's false sense of values in the conduct of their private lives. The restrained evening glow which suffuses the novel's last sentence has the quality of the final curtain at a theatrical performance: it also reflects a contentment of mind without which, surely, the narrator could never have undertaken his long exploration of the events and attitudes that led him and Estella to this final meeting in the deserted garden which is about to become the centre of re-building and new life. Despite its deflation of all except the most limited and old-fashioned expectations from human existence, the novel is a healing book.

Related though it was to Dickens's domestic problems the analysis of the springs of private happiness is not the novel's dominant concern. Dickens was pleased from the first with the aptness of his title, *Great Expectations*, and Lionel Trilling's interpretation of that approval is basically sound, though slightly exaggerated in emphasis: 'The greatness of *Great Expectations* begins in its title: modern society bases itself on great expectations which, if ever they are realised, are found to exist by reason of a sordid, hidden reality. The real thing is not the gentility of Pip's life but the hulks and the murder and the rats and decay in the cellarage of the novel.' Such a forthright interpretation does insufficient justice to Dickens's artistry, to his continuous attempts to keep telling the story as an act of Pip's mature and mellowed recollection; it removes Joe and Biddy to the margins of the tale and places Magwitch and Compeyson permanently in the central position. The novel has been so skilfully constructed out of a series of interlocking events and thematic convolutions, and the novelist seems to rely so heavily in the later scenes on actual echoes and recalls of earlier events, dialogues and situations, that no simple, unitary solution to its multiple meanings can be found completely acceptable. Monroe Engel has singled out for approval, as a sign of Dickens's increasing, conscious artistry in this novel, the manner in which 'plot, themes, symbols' from the public and private world 'all support each other'. For this reason, perhaps, some critics have expressed a vague dissastisfaction not only with the novel's ending, but also with the ambivalent attitude of Pip towards the events and characters of his story. It is no surprise that a similar ambivalence towards the novel is shown by a variety of critics and this suggests that, apart from certain obvious lessons (about hard work, the need for self-knowledge, and the essential rightness of old-fashioned domestic virtues), the novel raises more questions than it answers. Two major and two minor themes, however, are brought clearly before the reader's conscious mind before the novel ends: parasitism in public and private life is severely con-demned, and a large question mark is raised against the operations of human justice; in support of these indictments Dickens constantly reverts to the unfulfilled need for a true form of education that will act as a counterforce not only to the accidents of chance but, more signific-antly, to the consequences of heredity.

Analysis, based upon successive re-readings of the novel, can show the rigour with which Dickens stripped his theme to a few intellectual conceptions, but the reader still remembers that these basic ideas are surrounded by thousands of observed pieces of detail, innumerable remembered dialogues, and the novelist's own sense of the demands of his personal audience as well as the artistic demand that Pip should narrate his own story without much editorial prompting. The conse-quent accumulated store of concrete experiences, which upholds the narrative and extends its consequences in space and time, remains as vital and as meaningful a component in the total 'theme' of the novel as any intellectually isolable idea or effectively remembered symbol. It seems that Dickens's vivid awareness of the need to integrate such details into the central concept of his story never flags. When Mag-witch's fate is in the balance and the reader is quite certain that his cause is as doomed as his portable property is lost to Pip, the 'Jack' of the little causeway is then brought to our attention as one further, slimy comment on the acquisitive society. It is true that Pip treads the final path of purgation on the road to self-knowledge via the Blue Boar and the Forge; but this inn provides no congenial or convivial company, being but one more milestone on a journey, and the Forge (at least within the pages of the novel) is now only a symbol—no one is working there and the strains of 'Old Clem' have died out of the story. *Great Expectations* abounds in innumerable touches of this kind which suggest that, despite the occasional sentimentalism, the stretching of coincidence and the scarcely-concealed absence of any profound religious, moral or social formulation, Dickens was able to surround his fairy-tale story with so many echoes of nineteenth-century England that the reader is almost persuaded to accept his picture as the truth.

The present form of the ending of the novel acts powerfully and persuasively upon the reader. The original, discarded ending does not develop organically out of Pip's narrative: subsequent events are hastily telescoped together and presented in a manner that is quite external to the mood of the entire tale. It records a chance meeting with Estella in Piccadilly and ends with as tired a sentence as Dickens ever composed: 'I was very glad afterwards to have had the interview; for, in her face and in her voice, and in her touch, she gave me the assurance, that suffering had been stronger than Miss Havisham's teaching, and had given her a heart to Understand what my heart used to be.' The present ending is as completely integrated into the fable-like quality of the tale as it is surely grounded upon psychological perception; the dialogue and the narrative are freshly written and, through them, Dickens succeeds in reducing his complex material to its simplest terms, to Pip's sustained quest for personal fulfilment.

For the story eventually by-passes the world of public events and social themes, although these considerations have occupied large areas in the narrative. To our surprise the end of the third Stage leads us through the Forsaken Garden towards a far from Earthly Paradise which is expressed for us in curiously negative and tentative prose: 'and in all the broad expanse of tranquil light they showed to me, I saw no shadow of another parting from her'. Pip's explorations into things past which once seemed to threaten and expose the very foundations of law and order have not shaped him into a revolutionary, but given him these modified, subdued, yet acceptable grounds for hope in a future of domestic happiness. The novel is essentially a mid-Victorian masterpiece.

Additional Reading

I *Texts*

The Letters of Charles Dickens, 3 vols., Nonesuch Press (1938)
David Copperfield, O.U.P. (1952)
The Uncommercial Traveller and Reprinted Pieces, O.U.P. (1958)
The Uncollected Writings of Charles Dickens: Household Words 1850–1859, 2 vols., The Penguin Press (1968)

II *Biographical and Critical Studies*

Forster, J., *The Life of Charles Dickens* (1872-4)
Chesterton, G. K., *Charles Dickens* (1906)
—— *Appreciations and Criticisms of the Works of Charles Dickens* (1933)
Phillips, Walter C., *Dickens, Reade, and Collins*, New York (1919; 1962)
Dexter, W., *The Kent of Dickens* (1924)
—— *The London of Dickens* (1930)
Gissing, G., *The Immortal Dickens* (1925)
—— *Charles Dickens: A Critical Study* (1926)
Orwell, G., *Inside the Whale* (1940)
House, A. H., *The Dickens World* (1941)
Wilson, E., *The Wound and the Bow*, Boston (1941)
Shaw, G. B., *Introduction to Great Expectations* (1947)
Van O'Connor, W. (ed.), *Forms of Modern Fiction*, O.U.P. (1948)
Cruickshank, R. J., *Dickens and Early Victorian England* (1949)
Lindsay, J., *Dickens: A Biographical and Critical Study* (1950)
Trilling, L., *The Liberal Imagination*, London (1951)
—— *Introduction to 'Little Dorrit'*, O.U.P. (1953)
Johnson, E., *Dickens: His Tragedy and Triumph*, 2 vols., New York (1952)
Tillotson, K., *Novels of the Eighteen-Forties* (1954)
Ford, G. H., *Dickens and his Readers*, Princeton (1955)
Butt, J. and Tillotson, K., *Dickens at Work* (1957)
Miller, J. Hillis, *Charles Dickens: The World of his Novels* (1958)
Engel, Monroe, *The Maturity of Dickens* (1959)
Daiches, David, *The Novel and the Modern World* (1960)
Cockshut, A. O. J., *The Imagination of Charles Dickens* (1961)
Ford, G. H. and Lane, Lauriat (eds.), *The Dickens Critics*, New York (1961)

Gross, J. and Pearson, G. (eds.), *Dickens and the Twentieth Century* (1962)

Fielding, K. J., *Charles Dickens: A Critical Judgement*, 2nd edn. (1965)

Garis, R., *The Dickens Theatre: A Re-assessment of the Novels* (1965)

Dabney, Ross H., *Love and Property in the Novels of Dickens* (1967)

Dyson, A. E. (ed.), *Dickens: Modern Judgements* (1968)

Tomlin, E. W. F. (ed.), *Charles Dickens, 1812–1870: A Centenary Volume* (1969)

Brook, G. L., *The Language of Dickens* (1970)

Daleski, H. M., *Dickens and the Art of Analogy* (1970)

Dyson, A. E., *The Inimitable Dickens: A Reading of the Novels* (1970)

Hardy, Barbara, *The Moral Art of Dickens: essays* (1970)

Leavis, F. R. and Q. D., *Dickens the Novelist* (1970)

Lucas, John, *The Melancholy Man: A Study of Dickens's Novels* (1970)

Slater, Michael (ed.), *Dickens 1970: Centenary Essays* (1970)

Sucksmith, H. P., *The Narrative Art of Charles Dickens* (1970)

Wilson, *The World of Charles Dickens* (1970)

Manning, Sylvia, *Dickens as Satirist* [Yale Studies in English 176] (1971)

Watt, Ian (ed.), *The Victorian Novel: Modern Essays in Criticism* (1971)

III *Some Important Articles*

(a) In *Dickensian:*

Ford, F. Madox, *Great Expectations* and its early readers (1940)

House, H., G. B. Shaw on *Great Expectations* (1948)

Butt, J., Dickens's Plan for the Conclusion of *Great Expectations* (1949)

Morley, M., Stages of *Great Expectations* (1955)

Drew, A. P., Structure in *Great Expectations* (1956)

Fielding, K. J., Weekly Serialisation (1958)

Clinton-Baddeley, V. C., "Wopsle" (1961)

Centenary number (1970)

(b) In *Nineteenth-Century Fiction:*

Rouse, H. B., Charles Dickens and Henry James: Two approaches to Fiction, V (1950)

Hagan, J. H., The Poor Labyrinth: The Theme of Social Injustice in *Great Expectations*, IX (1954)

Edminson, M., The Date of the Action in *Great Expectations*, XIII (1958)

Raleigh, J. H., Dickens and the Sense of Time, XIII (1958)

Levine, George, Communications in *Great Expectations* (1963)

(c) Other Articles

Van Ghent, Dorothy, The Dickens World, *Sewannee Review*, LVIII (1950)

Hagan, J. H., Structural Patterns in Dickens's *Great Expectations*, *E.L.H.*, XXI (1954)

Connolly, T. E., Technique in *Great Expectations*, *Philological Quarterly*, XXXIV (1955)

Cox, C. B., In Defence of Dickens, *Essays and Studies* (1958)

Fielding, K. J., The Critical Autonomy of *Great Expectations*, R.E.S. (1961)

Hynes, Joseph A., Image and Symbol in *Great Expectations*, J.E.LH. (1963)

Marcus, Philip L., Theme and Suspense in the Plot of *Great Expectations*, Dickens Stu. ̄s (1966)

Partlow, Robert B. (ed.), *Dickens Studies Annual*, Vol. I (1970)

Collins, Philip (ed.), Dickens [The Critical Heritage Series] (1971)

Index